Literature

# Literature

Amos Paran and Pauline Robinson

OXFORD
UNIVERSITY PRESS

# OXFORD
### UNIVERSITY PRESS

Great Clarendon Street, Oxford, OX2 6DP, United Kingdom

Oxford University Press is a department of the University of Oxford.
It furthers the University's objective of excellence in research, scholarship,
and education by publishing worldwide. Oxford is a registered trade
mark of Oxford University Press in the UK and in certain other countries

ISBN: 978 0 19 442752 4

Printed in China

This book is printed on paper from certified and well-managed sources

ACKNOWLEDGEMENTS

*The authors and publisher are grateful to those who have given permission to reproduce
the following extracts and adaptations of copyright material*: p.15 Extract from
"Ridgways Imperial Blend" advertisement, 1983. Reproduced by permission
of Typhoo Tea Limited. p.17 "This Is Just to Say" by William Carlos Williams,
from *The Collected Poems: Volume 1, 1909–1939*, copyright © 1938 by New
Directions Publishing Corp. Reprinted by permission of New Directions
Publishing Corp. and Carcanet Press Limited. p.77 "Superman" from *Collected
Poems, 1953–1993* by John Updike (Hamish Hamilton 1993), copyright © 1993
by John Updike. Used by permission of Penguin Books Ltd and Alfred A. Knopf,
an imprint of Knopf Doubleday Publishing Group, a division of Penguin
Random House LLC. All rights reserved. p.82 "Horse" from *The Collected Poems
of George Mackay Brown* edited by Archie Bevan and Brian Murray (John Murray
Press, 2006). Copyright © 2005 Estate of George Mackay Brown. Reproduced
by permission of John Murray Press, an imprint of Hodder and Stoughton
Limited. p.83 "A Song Before Marriage" from *The Dove and the Leopard* by W. G.
Archer (Orient Longmans Ltd., 1948). Reproduced with permission of Orient
Blackswan Pvt Ltd. p.86 "What Has Happened to Lulu?" by Charles Causley
from *Collected Poems 1951–2000* (Macmillan, 1992). Reproduced by permission
of David Higham Associated Limited. p.94–5 Excerpt from *The Curious Incident
Of The Dog In The Night-Time: A Novel* by Mark Haddon, copyright © 2003 by
Mark Haddon. Published by David Fickling Books. Used by permission of
The Random House Group Limited and Doubleday, an imprint of the Knopf
Doubleday Publishing Group, a division of Penguin Random House LLC. All
rights reserved. p.23,110–1 Extracts from "Blood Knot" from *Selected Plays* by
Athol Fugard (Oxford University Press, 1987). Reproduced by permission of
Oxford University Press. p.23,114–5 Extracts from "The Ash Girl" from *Plays 2*
by Timberlake Wertenbaker (Faber & Faber Limited, 2000) © Timberlake
Wertenbaker 2000. Reproduced by permission of Faber & Faber Limited.
p.129 "Musée des Beaux Arts", copyright © 1940 and renewed 1968 by
W. H. Auden; *W. H. Auden Collected Poems* by W. H. Auden. Used by permission
of Curtis Brown and Random House, an imprint and division of Penguin
Random House LLC. All rights reserved. p.130 "Musea voor Schone Kunsten"
from *On the Lookout* by Jeremy Kingston (Hearing Eye, 2008). Reproduced

by permission of Jeremy Kingston. p.133 Page from *Great Expectations: The
Graphic Novel* by Charles Dickens (Classical Comics, 2009). Reproduced by
permission of Classical Comics. p.17 Note by Tim Flannery on "This Is Just
to Say", reproduced by permission of Tim Flannery, note by Michael Tagle
on "This Is Just to Say", reproduced by permission of Michael Tagle. p.31–2
Note by Sarah Wray on "If" reproduced by permission of Sarah Wray, note by
Robert Rose on "If" reproduced by permission of Robert Rose, note by Dinky
Davis on "If" reproduced by permission of Dinky Davis, note by Nicole Rose
on "If" reproduced by permission of Nicole Rose, note by Susan Rose-Wray
on "If" reproduced by permission of Susan Rose-Wray. p.67–8 Note by Oded
Amir on "The Kiss" reproduced by permission of Oded Amir, note by Dinky
Davis on "The Kiss" reproduced by permission of Dinky Davis, note by Nicole
Rose on "The Kiss" reproduced by permission of Nicole Rose, note by Sarah
Wray on "The Kiss" reproduced by permission of Sarah Wray, note by Robert
Rose on "The Kiss" reproduced by permission of Robert Rose, note by Fergus
Backhouse on "The Kiss" reproduced by permission of Fergus Backhouse.
p.135 Note by Oded Amir on "Full Fathom Five" reproduced by permission
of Oded Amir. "How Soon Can I Leave?" from *A Bit of Singing and Dancing* by
Susan Hill, published by Long Barn Books © Susan Hill 2013. Reproduced
online by permission of Sheil Land Associates Ltd. p.92 cover 1 (red, white
dog); artwork copyright Mark Boutevant, Suzanne Dean and Tim Marrs; used
by arrangement with The Random House Group Limited. p.92 cover 2 (blue
artwork); artwork copyright Henry Steadman; used by arrangement with The
Random House Group.

*Sources*: p.20 "Lunch with the FT: Katherine Boo" by Jan Dalley, www.ft.com,
14 November 2014. p.93 *Haroun and the Sea of Stories* by Rushdie Salman
(Granta, 1990). p.53 *The Brooklyn Follies* by Paul Auster (Faber & Faber Limited,
2011). p.40 *Edwin Arlington Robinson* by Emery Neff (Methuen Publishing, 1949).
p.40 *Tendencies in Modern American Poetry* by Amy Lowell (Houghton Mifflin
Company, 1917). p.40 Edwin Arlington Robinson by Yvor Winters (New
Directions Publishing Corp., 1946).

We would like to dedicate this book to our colleagues at CALS, the Centre for Applied Language Studies at the University of Reading, where we first met and where we first taught the courses on literature in the EFL classroom that have led to this book.

# Acknowledgements

Special thanks go to Sophie Rogers, who accompanied us in the main part of this project, and whose faith in the book supported us throughout. Thanks are also due to Cathy Kneafsey, Keith Laycock, Julia Bell and Caroline Chappell for their support at different stages. Andrew Dilger was a sensitive and knowledgeable editor, who understood what we were seeking to do, listened to our requests and found ways of accommodating them. We owe him a huge amount of gratitude.

Over the years we have benefited immensely from attending workshops and from reading and consulting the work of Michael Benson, Chris Brumfit, Ron Carter, Joanne Collie, Guy Cook, Alan Durant, Gillian Lazar, Michael Long, Alan Maley, John McRae, Rob Pope, Alan Pulverness, Stephen Slater, Jane Spiro and many others. Many of the ideas in this book have evolved from engaging with the work of these colleagues.

Amos would like to acknowledge Avigail Kirschenbaum Noy, who was the creator of some of the activities for *Richard Cory* and *The Parable of the Old Man and the Young*, exemplified in this book. Pauline would like to thank Rose and Dan Renshaw for suggesting the use of *An Arrest* by Ambrose Bierce. She would also like to thank the British Council for sponsoring her involvement in courses, conferences and consultancies around the world over the years, focusing either on ESP or on the teaching of literature. We would like to thank Oded Amir, Fergus Backhouse, Dinky Davis, Tim Flannery, Susan Rose, Robert Rose, Nicole Rose, Michael Tagle, and Sarah Wray, whose reactions to our prompts appear in some of the activities. Many thanks to Jeremy Kingston for kindly allowing us to reprint his poem *Musea voor Schone Kunsten*.

Finally, both of us would like to express our thanks to the EFL teachers on the various courses on literature and language teaching we have taught over the years, but especially to the teachers who attended our courses on using literature in French Lycées which we co-taught for many years, and who have contributed so much to our thinking and our knowledge.

# Contents

# Introduction

## Who this book is for

If you have picked up this book, it is because you are interested in using literature in your classrooms – or perhaps you already do. You probably love literature, and want to pass this love on to your learners as well, but wonder how you can bring literature into your classroom and integrate it with modern, 21st century pedagogy and methodologies. This is precisely the issue that we have grappled with in our teaching and teacher-training careers, and is what we explore in this book.

Your learners are no doubt improving their grasp of the English language and may even be at an intermediate level or above. They may be learning English primarily because it is a subject in the curriculum, or they may in fact be studying English literature itself. As their teacher, you may be required to follow a particular textbook, or you may have some choice. Your primary aim may be to work on the learners' linguistic improvement, or to broaden and deepen their understanding and knowledge of literature in English, or more generally, to help with learners' personal development. Whatever your purposes, we hope that you can find time to incorporate some literary texts into your syllabus, using some of the pieces that we present here and trying out some of the activities that we suggest.

Together, we have many years' experience around the world teaching teachers both of language and of literature, teaching college and university lecturers, and teaching students in schools, colleges, and universities. We have worked in the UK, most of the European countries, Israel, the Middle East, Africa, Malaysia, Thailand, China, Japan, and South America. The many students and teachers that we have worked with have helped us to develop the ideas we present.

While we are both trained teachers of English language, we love literature and see it as a wonderful resource for teaching language. Some might see literature as difficult, both in terms of language use and of content. Until the 1960s or so, however, it was normal to use literary texts in English language textbooks. Then along came the ESP (English for Specific Purposes) revolution, which used material from learners' specialist areas of interest, for example, agriculture, economics, or science. Many of these texts were difficult for teachers, but techniques were developed to cope with them. Some of these techniques, it was realized, could be used with literary material. The wheel has come full circle.

## How this book is organized

Throughout this book, we have made sure that we provide you with a wide range of practical ideas and activities while at the same time giving some theoretical background and a rationale for using them.

The book is organized in three parts. In Part 1 (Chapters 1–3), we consider in a general way the issues of language and literature in the EFL classroom. Chapter 1 explores issues of literature and literary language, focusing also on learners and their reactions, and the way in which learners can be involved in classroom activities and choices. Chapter 2 looks at different approaches and techniques for the use of literature in the EFL classroom. Chapter 3 considers what readers (or learners) bring to a text, looking at how reading and discussing literature interact with our knowledge of the world and of other literary works. Part 2 then looks at the four major **genres** of literature – short stories, poems, novels, and drama – and focuses on the specific issues that arise when working with each of them. Finally, Part 3 links literature with other art forms: film (Chapter 8) and visual art and music (Chapter 9).

## How to use this book

Although there are many links between the chapters in the book, you do not need to read it from beginning to end. Each chapter can be read on its own, though Part 1 does provide a good overall view of our approach and will give you tools and techniques that you can use with many different literary works.

The main text of the book deals with a large variety of literary texts, in some cases providing example lesson sequences for specific works. However, the activities are often not tied down to specific texts, but are there for you to take and experiment with on other texts as well. *Try this* activities provide you with specific ideas and techniques that you can try immediately with a variety of works. *Getting it right* sections give procedural tips for some of our more specific suggestions. *Why this works* sections provide a pedagogic rationale for many of the activities. In addition, there is a *Glossary* for words which appear in bold in the main text, and a list of *Useful websites* for extending or developing activities online. Within the book, we refer to extra downloadable resources on the accompanying website. These can be found at: www.oup.com/elt/teacher/itc

We hope you will feel able to dip into the book for ideas, tips, and inspiration for specific works, or to help you with the works in your own syllabus, as well as for a rounded, sustained understanding of the many ways in which literature can be brought to life in the EFL classroom.

# Part 1    Establishing the groundwork

# 1 Literature and language in the EFL classroom

## Why use literature in the EFL classroom?

Why should we spend our learners' time on literature when there is much more that seems more useful to learners? What is the relevance of literature to our learners' lives?

The answer to these questions can be found in the way in which literature is in fact part of all of our lives, and we start this chapter with an example in which a non-literary figure illustrates the role of literature in her own life.

In 2010, the Harveian Oration at the Royal College of Physicians in the UK was delivered by Dr Iona Heath. She started her oration by saying:

> I bring nearly 35 years of experience of trying to make my grasp of biomedical science useful to the astonishingly diverse population of … north London. And in *Mrs Dalloway* Virginia Woolf describes one of the compensations of growing old as being 'the power of taking hold of experience, of turning it round, slowly, in the light'.

Here is a prestigious annual lecture on medicine, which in the second sentence refers to one of the most important literary works of the 20th century.

Literature, then, is part of the human experience and using literature in our language teaching does not take away from our learners' language learning. Rather, it builds connections that are made elsewhere in our learners' future professions; it enriches their learning; and it also increases their knowledge of an important part of the culture of English-speaking countries.

A potential objection to literature in the language classroom is that learners may not be able to cope with such texts, and that pedagogic texts (texts specially produced for teaching purposes) are better for them. We hope that the choice of texts for this book will show not only that there are texts which learners are capable of dealing with, but also that it is possible to construct teaching and learning activities for these texts. We also hope the texts suggested in this book are entertaining and enjoyable, and can promote language practice and development.

## Exploring the meaning of literature

Learners often think of literature as something that is remote from them and not part of their lives, but we are all exposed to literature and literary texts. This section aims to help learners realize what they already know about literature. Learners may also have fixed ideas about what is literature and what is not. However, there is no obvious dividing line between literary and non-literary texts – rather, it is a continuum. There are texts that are clearly literary and texts that are non-literary, but there are also many non-literary texts with literary uses of language, or literary texts where we can't easily pinpoint why they are literary. We explore this continuum below, with the purpose of helping learners to refine their own ideas of what they believe to be literature and, hopefully, broaden their enjoyment of it.

### Getting learners to think about literary and non-literary texts

The first text we present is in fact an advertisement, which illustrates the way in which poetic language can occur in a range of texts.

Rather than asking learners 'What is literature?', it is easier to start with a more focused discussion of 'What is poetry?' Even people who claim not to like poetry usually have some ideas about what a poem is like. As a preliminary activity, get students to discuss – either in small groups or as a whole class – the question of 'What is poetry?' using their experience of English and of their own language. Ask them what a poem is. What does it look like? Do we usually read it or listen to it? What features does it often have?

Answers might include that a poem has a special shape or layout on the page, that it uses **rhyme** for some or all of the lines, that there is usually a distinctive **rhythm**, and that there may be unusual vocabulary which helps to create colourful and unusual images. Experience and opinions can vary, of course, and there is no right answer, only a developing awareness and sensitivity to these features and poetry in general. Text 1.1, which is an advert for tea, illustrates these points.

---

### New from Ridgways.

An Imperial Blend of high-grown teas from the fabled gardens of Assam and Sri Lanka.

Refreshing. Fragrant. Full-bodied.
A tea to bewitch your bleak afternoons.
A tea to solace your midnights.
A tea to welcome your mornings.

**Ridgways Imperial Blend**
*Unmistakably, a tea of character. In packets or teabags.*

---

TEXT 1.1    *Advert for Ridgways Imperial Blend*

The text, originally in colour, was superimposed on an image of a bone-china teacup and saucer containing rich brown tea, with gold-plated sugar tongs poised above, holding a lump of sugar. Most students will spot that the last line clearly shows the text to be an advert for tea, whether loose or as teabags. The first phrase identifies the company.

Ask students, in groups or as a whole class, to consider the text in the light of the discussion on the nature of poetry. Use the following questions, to which we suggest some answers in brackets.

### Questions

1   Is there anything special about the layout?
    (No – it is in continuous **prose**, not in separate lines like most poems.)

2   Is there rhyme or rhythm?
    (No. However, there are some patterns of sound. The words 'fabled', 'refreshing', 'fragrant', and 'full-bodied' each begin with, or have as the second syllable, the sound /f/ or /fr/. This repetition of an initial or near initial consonant or consonant cluster is **alliteration**, a common technique in poetry. The shared sound suggests a link in the meaning of the words.)

3   Is there unusual vocabulary?
    (Yes, and this vocabulary conjures up many images. The advert is aimed at a British readership, and it includes names which for this audience are far-off, exotic places: Assam and Sri Lanka. Together with the reference to 'fabled' these may elicit mysterious, wonderful notions. There is also a reference to 'gardens', a word which normally has a very positive connotation, suggesting greenness, restfulness and beauty: feelings which we can transfer to the text.)

4   Are there any repeated grammatical patterns?
    (Yes, there is a series of almost identical phrases consisting of *a tea to* + verb + *your* + noun phrase. This kind of repetition of grammatical structure is known as **parallelism**. The noun phrases here move in time from afternoon to morning. The first two verbs ('bewitch', 'solace') are not so common and so perhaps poetic; the last one ('welcome') is more everyday.)

This advertising text clearly uses several poetic features: allusive language, sound patterning and grammatical patterning. We might also consider the presentation of phrases punctuated as sentences to be a fairly common feature of poetry. Why wouldn't we consider this advertising copy to be poetry, then? Primarily because its function is to direct us to action, in this case to buy Ridgways teas, rather than to delight and entertain us or to express the writer's feelings.

---

**Try this** ☞ **Poetic language in adverts**

Adverts with poetic features can be found in most societies. Adverts selling cars, cosmetics, holidays, fashion, or food are likely candidates.
- Collect adverts in your L1 and discuss them in class.
- Collect some adverts in English and analyse them in the same way.
- Ask students to collect adverts with poetic features, either in L1 or in English.
- Ask them to describe or list the poetic features in the adverts that have been collected and brought to class.

---

**Try this** ☞ **Students as copywriters**

Get a range of pictures of consumer objects (e.g. cars, clothing, food items). Ask students to write advertising headlines for them. Emphasize that these don't have to be grammatical sentences; creative headlines and slogans often break the rules of Standard English!

As a contrasting example, let's look at a poem which, like the advert (Text 1.1), seems to blur the boundaries between literary and non-literary language.

> **This is Just to Say**
>
> I have eaten
> the plums
> that were in
> the icebox
>
> and which
> you were probably
> saving
> for breakfast
>
> Forgive me
> they were delicious
> so sweet
> and so cold

TEXT 1.2    This Is Just To Say *(1934) by William Carlos Williams*

This is a famous poem which many people enjoy because they love the image of the plums, the simplicity of the language, and the development and apparent inevitability of the message. The longer line, 'they were delicious', also contrasts with the brevity and conciseness of the last two lines, with the conclusiveness of their final hard /t/ and /d/ (both plosive consonants).

Other readers are irritated by the poem because it seems unpoetic, with simple (even simplistic) everyday language and mundane content. If it were not written in short lines – as poems usually are – but as a continuous passage, surely it could just as well be the text of a note on the fridge? In fact, comparing the poem with the way people would actually convey the message highlights the poetic qualities of the text. Texts 1.3 and 1.4 are texts which two people (who did not know the poem) produced in response to the prompt 'Write a short note to apologize for eating fruit from the fridge – for example, plums':

| | |
|---|---|
| Michael – finished the plums – Sorry! I'll get more.<br>T. | I've had your prunes. Will replace them in the morning. I love you. |

TEXTS 1.3 AND 1.4    *Notes in response to prompt*

Though we often think of poetry as being more concise than speech, it is interesting that the poem is more explicit than the notes are. The poem adds detail that is not relevant to apologizing – the two notes make it clear that the fruit will be replaced, whereas the poem focuses on the taste of the plums. Note also that there is no punctuation anywhere in the poem, which both notes have. Although the poem has a title, it is in fact grammatically part of the poem itself. So, like the tea advert, this poem illustrates the point that the language of a poem may not be obviously marked as literary or poetic. Importantly, it also shows that it is attempting to do something different from the notes: the point is not to apologize, or to promise to replace the plums; the poem simply delights in the fruit, its freshness and its taste – and delights in itself.

**Try this** 👉   **Continuous text vs. line breaks**

Give Text 1.2 to students as one line of continuous text and ask them to write it out as if it were a poem. Then compare their suggestions with the actual poem, asking for possible ideas as to why the poet chose the line breaks in the way he did.

**Try this** 👉   **Comparing poetic qualities**

Ask students to compare and contrast Text 1.1 with Text 1.2. Which one do they think is more poetic and why? Which one do they prefer?

**Try this** 👉   **Creative writing**

Ask students to try writing short poems about food items that they like, in the style of either Text 1.1. or 1.2. Display their work as posters in the classroom.

**Try this** 👉   **What is/isn't a poem?**

Ask students to look at short poems which exhibit different elements of literariness. Which of them would/wouldn't they consider to be a poem? What are they basing their judgement on? Possible choices are *I always eat peas with honey*, a jokey short verse; *What am I after all?* by Walt Whitman, which exhibits his use of **free verse** and a conversational tone; and WB Yeats' *Down by the Salley Gardens*, with its folk song elements. Make sure that you also include one or two poems which conform more than the others to what learners would think of as poetry. (You can find the Yeats and Whitman poems by going to the website of Project Gutenberg, which includes a large number of texts which are out of copyright. The website address can be found in Useful websites, page 139.)

**Why this works** ▷   **Verbalizing implicit knowledge**

The activities above help students to verbalize what they implicitly know about literature and literary texts. They help them realize that literature is not always highbrow, but that it can be humorous, light-hearted, and indeed sometimes trivial. It can break rules and play with them.

**Try this** 👉   **Humorous and nonsense verse**

Ask students to find humorous and **nonsense verse** in their L1 and bring it to class. Discuss how their examples compare with any examples you have looked at with them.

✔ *Getting it right*   **What students think**

Make sure that you elicit from students what they think, rather than telling them what acceptable answers are. In fact, discussion is likely to reveal that students have quite clear ideas about what poems are normally like and about poetic language. Accepting their points of view is likely to result in their experiencing a sense of freedom and creativity: poems and other printed texts don't always have to have complete sentences; poems don't have to have elevated subject matter.

## Exploring literature as a secondary world

### Describing people

Part of what happens in literature is the creation of a new world. An aspect of the experience of reading (discussed in Chapter 2) is for readers to immerse themselves in this new world conjured up by the novelist, short story writer, poet, or playwright. The new world which the writer has created has to be peopled by characters (mostly human but also animals or invented beings such as vampires, elves, ghosts, or aliens). These characters inhabit a physical world, houses and landscapes, which need to be described.

It is possible to construct an exercise for thinking about 'literariness' by looking at prose texts. Ask students to look at Texts 1.5–1.7, three descriptions of people. Show the texts to the students without revealing their sources, and ask them to think about the following questions.

### Questions
1 What physical features are focused on?
2 What is the purpose of the extract?
3 Who is narrating the extract?
4 How reliable is the narrator?
5 Which extract do you prefer? Which person would you like to read more about?
6 Which are literary texts, and which are not? How do you know?

> Along the road walked an old man. He was white-headed as a mountain, bowed in the shoulders and faded in general aspect. He wore a glazed hat, an ancient boat-cloak, and shoes; his brass buttons bearing an anchor upon their face. In his hand was a silver-headed walking-stick, which he used as a veritable third leg, perseveringly dotting the ground with its point at every few inches' interval. One would have said that he had been, in his day, a naval officer of some sort or other.

TEXT 1.5    *Extract from Chapter 2 of* The Return of the Native *(1878) by Thomas Hardy*

> Setting my eyes on Mr Wemmick as we went along, to see what he was like in the light of day, I found him to be a dry man, rather short in stature, with a square wooden face, whose expression seemed to have been imperfectly chipped-out in a dull-edged chisel. There were some marks in it that might have been dimples, if the material had been softer and the instrument finer, but which as it was, were only dints. The chisel had made three or four of these attempts at embellishment over his nose, but had given them up without an effort to smooth them.

TEXT 1.6    *Extract from Chapter 21 of* Great Expectations *(1860–61) by Charles Dickens*

> [Katharine] Boo, tiny, frail and with an immune system that is not on her side, hardly seems a person who should be in an environment like Annawadi's, where tuberculosis is rife … her moon-blonde hair and china-white skin must have made her seem like a being from another planet.

TEXT 1.7    *Extract from interview in* Financial Times *(2014)*

In Text 1.5, there is an attempt to provide a fairly complete description with many literal details, and then distil certain qualities from the description. In Text 1.6, rather than attempting a full description, Dickens provides a **metaphorical** one. Text 1.7, taken from an interview with American journalist, Katharine Boo, focuses on only one aspect of her appearance, her frailty, mainly in the context of her work in Mumbai.

## Describing places

Many literary works contain descriptions of cities, buildings, and natural features, some of which may be real. These descriptions will differ from those typically found in guidebooks or geography books, because the writers' purposes are different. Writers of guidebooks must provide clear factual information, although sometimes they may use the **entertainment function**, in order to encourage readers to visit the places described. Novelists will also use the entertainment function, and probably the **poetic function**, too. They will be less concerned about providing a complete description of place, as they are focused on what is important to their characters. (See below for a more detailed discussion of the different literary functions.)

---

**Try this** ☞   **Comparing play sets**

Choose three or four descriptions of the **set** from different plays (e.g. Victorian dramatists usually include detailed descriptions of the set, as do modern playwrights such as Alan Ayckbourn, Arthur Miller and Peter Shaffer; other modern writers such as Samuel Beckett and Harold Pinter have very sparse descriptions). Give the various descriptions to your students to compare. What is the effect of the additional detail? Does it help? What does each description suggest about the play?

---

**Try this** ☞   **Comparing real-life settings with fictional descriptions**

Many novelists use real buildings as an inspiration for fictional settings. Chatsworth House, in Derbyshire, is thought to be the inspiration for Pemberley, Mr Darcy's house in Jane Austen's *Pride and Prejudice*. Madresfield Court in Worcestershire is the inspiration for Evelyn Waugh's *Brideshead Revisited*. Kings Cross station in London features in many works of literature, such as EM Forster's *Howards End* and more recently the *Harry Potter* series. Ask students to find information online about the real-life locations and compare what they have learnt with the literary depictions.

---

**Try this** ☞   **Cities in literature vs. cities in guides**

Ask students to compare descriptions of cities in literary works with descriptions of these cities in guidebooks or on tourist websites. Good sources are Charles Dickens' *A Tale of Two Cities* (Paris and London), George Orwell's *Down and Out in Paris and London*, and Paul Auster's *The New York Trilogy*.

## Functions of language

As we noted in our discussion of the Ridgways tea advert in Text 1.1, the function of a text plays an important part in our reception of it. The advertisement has poetic features, but it has an advertising function. A humorous poem about eating peas is hardly great poetry, but it clearly fulfils a very different purpose from the advert – its aim is to entertain. The different descriptions of people in Texts 1.5–1.7 also have different functions. Clearly, helping learners appreciate the different functions of language helps sensitize them to the nature of literature and literary language.

The list of functions below, which is a fairly standard one, may be helpful when thinking about working with literary and non-literary texts. It can be a tool to talk about texts and help differentiate their effects.

1 **Directive function**: The speaker/writer tries to get other people to do something. For example:

| | |
|---|---|
| Commands: | Get out! |
| | Be quiet! |
| Request: | Could you help me lift this, please? |
| Suggestion: | Why don't you try again? |

2 **Informational function**: The speaker/writer gives or requests information. The focus is on the content or meaning. For example:

| | |
|---|---|
| Statements: | It's Mary's birthday today. |
| | It's raining. |
| Question: | Where's the railway station? |

3 **Expressive function**: The speaker or writer presents their feelings and attitudes, possibly without regard for the effect on the listeners and readers. For example:

Statement: I love ice cream.
Exclamation: Phew! I'm exhausted!
Exclamation/rhetorical question: Wow! Isn't it hot today?

4 **Interactional function**: Also known as the **phatic function**. The main purpose is to create, develop, and maintain social contact and cohesion between the people involved. For example:

A: Hi, how are you?
B: Great. You?
A: Not bad. Good film last night, wasn't it?
B: Yeah – really good.
A: Yeah.

5 **Poetic function**: Also called the **aesthetic function**. The focus is on the actual forms of language used. Information or emotion may be conveyed, but the speaker/writer very clearly intends the listener/reader to appreciate and be aware of the actual linguistic choice: perhaps for the sound quality, the playfulness or wit, etc. This function is most evident in poetry and other creative writing, but it is not confined to them. A major use of the poetic function is in adverts, as in the one for Ridgways tea in Text 1.1.

6 **Metalingual function**: This focuses on the use of language itself. It is less common and mainly used by linguists and language teachers. It typically combines with the informational function, allowing the speaker/writer to question and give information on the forms of language being used. For example:

A: This should be done by Thursday.

B: What are you saying here? Are you giving an order or just being hopeful?

7 **Entertainment function**: The word 'entertainment' here has a wide scope, and refers to the enjoyment which the text provides for the listener/reader. This can range from the enjoyment readers get from horror stories to romantic novels or humour and **comedy**. This function is particularly relevant when we are considering literature.

**Try this** ☞ **Identifying functions in a single extract**

Ask students to study the following extract from the play *The Importance of Being Earnest* by Oscar Wilde (considered further in Chapter 7). Jack Worthing is hoping to propose to Gwendolen Fairfax, who is the daughter of Lady Bracknell. The extract starts with the first words Jack speaks after they are left alone.

Ask students, in pairs or small groups, to identify the functions of Jack and Gwendolen's utterances. This analysis helps them understand the way in which the extract is funny: on a superficial level it observes the conversational protocol, while at the same time challenging it.

| | |
|---|---|
| **Jack** | Charming day it has been, Miss Fairfax. |
| **Gwendolen** | Pray don't talk to me about the weather, Mr Worthing. Whenever people talk to me about the weather, I always feel quite certain that they mean something else. And that makes me so nervous. |
| **Jack** | I do mean something else. |
| **Gwendolen** | I thought so. In fact, I am never wrong. |
| **Jack** | And I would like to be allowed to take advantage of Lady Bracknell's temporary absence— |
| **Gwendolen** | I would certainly advise you to do so. Mamma has a way of coming back suddenly into a room that I have often had to speak to her about. |

TEXT 1.8    *Extract from* The Importance of Being Earnest *(1895) by Oscar Wilde*

**Try this** ☞ **Identifying functions in quotations**

Ask students to examine the following quotations from plays referred to in Chapter 7 (some of which have been modified or paraphrased). Which functions do they think the quotations are performing? The answers are given in brackets.

- Tell Orsino not to send me any more messages. (*Twelfth Night* – directive function)
- I hate shoes, they squeeze my feet. (*The Ashgirl* – expressive function)
- I scorn your words, sir! (*The Lucky Chance* – expressive function)
- More of your money and less of your civility, good Sir. (*The Lucky Chance* – expressive and directive functions)

- Judith:    Fields of brocade.
  Ruth:      Cascades of lace.
  Judith:    Camelot.
  Ruth:      Chiffon.
  Judith:    The coolness of satin.
  (*The Ashgirl* – informational and poetic functions)
- I cannot love Orsino. (*Twelfth Night* – expressive function)
- Morris:      Hell, man, I often wonder.
  Zachariah:  Same here.
  Morris:      I mean where do they go, the good times, in a man's life?
  Zachariah:  And the bad ones?
  (*Blood Knot* – interactional function)

## Dialogue in literature and in real life

In the world that the writer creates, characters need to communicate with each other, so the writer needs to simulate dialogue as well. This raises the question of the extent to which speech in literary texts is like speech in real life, especially that of natural conversation.

**Try this** ☞    **Features of conversation**

Table 1.1 lists some of the typical features of natural conversation, with examples. Ask students which of these could occur in plays, short stories, and novels. Which might not? Are there any other features which might occur in literary texts? Delete some of the comments in the third column, and present the table to students for discussion.

| Feature | Example | Effect if used in literary texts |
| --- | --- | --- |
| Hesitation | Yes, er, well, I um, I am not sure how to say this … er … | Too much use of these features would make the text difficult to follow. |
| Reformulation | Yes, I went on Tuesday, ah no, it was Monday, no, let me see, I did in on Sunday. | |
| Incomplete elements | So, let's … erm I mean shall we … or what do you think? | |
| Overlapping speech | Two people speaking together, because enthusiastic or perhaps arguing. | |
| Turn-taking speech | A: Shall we go for a walk by the river?<br>B: Yes, let's. It's pretty, isn't it? | In plays we can also find monologues and soliloquies, as in *Hamlet*, for example. |
| Echoing speech | A: It was good, wasn't it?<br>B: Yes, it was very good. | This is usually done more poetically in plays or in fiction. |
| Use of verse | In *Macbeth*, Macbeth and Lady Macbeth speak in verse, whereas the Porter speaks in prose. | In older plays, use of verse identifies a main character. |
| Use of formal language | In *Jane Eyre*, Chapter 20, Mr Rochester gives Jane a rose and says: 'Do you like this sunrise, Jane? – that sky with its high and light clouds which are sure to melt away as the day waxes warm – this placid and balmy atmosphere?' | The language in older works of literature can seem formal and old-fashioned today. |
| Vague or inaccurate vocabulary | I saw old whatshisname the other day, you know old so-and-so. | Vocabulary in older pieces of literature is normally carefully selected. |

TABLE 1.1    *Features of conversation*

**Try this** ☞   **Researching natural speech**

Ask students to choose an interesting topic and record themselves discussing it. They should then listen to the recording and identify features that they find in their speech. Are there many hesitations, reformulations, etc? How much must the speech be 'tidied up' if it is to be written down as drama? (You can also make the point by asking your students to record themselves in their L1.)

**Try this** ☞   **Examining dialogue**

Ask students to look at the extract from the short story by DH Lawrence in Text 1.9. Explain the context: two sisters are discussing their adopted brother, Hadrian, who lives in Canada and has come to visit them and their father. The sisters' relationship with Hadrian has always been distant, possibly difficult, and they have always insisted that he should call them 'Cousin'.

---

'Do you want something to eat?'

Hadrian looked round – as if for the meal.

'I don't mind,' he said.

'What shall you have – egg and bacon?' asked Emmie shortly.

'Yes, I don't mind,' said Hadrian.

The sisters went down to the kitchen, and sent the servant to finish the stairs.

'Isn't he *altered*?' said Matilda, *sotto voce*.

'Isn't he!' said Cousin Emmie. '*What* a little man!'

They both made a grimace, and laughed nervously.

'Get the frying-pan,' said Emmie to Matilda.

'But he's as cocky as ever,' said Matilda, narrowing her eyes and shaking her head knowingly, as she handed the frying-pan.

'Mannie!' said Emmie sarcastically. Hadrian's new-fledged, cock-sure manliness evidently found no favour in her eyes.

'Oh, he's not bad,' said Matilda. 'You don't want to be prejudiced against him.'

'I'm not prejudiced against him, I think he's all right for looks,' said Emmie, 'but there's too much of the little mannie about him.'

'Fancy catching us like this,' said Matilda.

'They've no thought for anything,' said Emmie with contempt. 'You go up and get dressed, our Matilda. I don't care about him. I can see to things, and you can talk to him. I shan't.'

'He'll talk to my father,' said Matilda, meaningful.

'*Sly*-!' exclaimed Emmie, with a grimace.

The sisters believed that Hadrian had come hoping to get something out of their father – hoping for a legacy. And they were not at all sure he would not get it.

---

TEXT 1.9   *Extract from* Hadrian or You Touched Me *(1920) by DH Lawrence*

Ask students how Lawrence makes the dialogue dramatic. What 'stage directions' is he, in effect, providing? Get students to underline and categorize them as in Table 1.2.

| Feature | Example from *Hadrian* |
|---------|------------------------|
| Adverb | shortly, sarcastically |
| Adverbial phrase | *sotto voce*, with contempt, with a grimace |
| Adjective | meaningful |
| Description of sound or of physical gesture or movement | They made a grimace and laughed nervously Narrowing her eyes and shaking her head |
| Typographical device (e.g. italics) | Isn't he *altered*? |
| Exclamation | *What* a little man! |

TABLE 1.2    *Ways of making dialogue dramatic*

**Try this** ☞     **Reporting dialogue**

Brainstorm words with a similar meaning to 'said' with students. In Text 1.9, there is just one alternative: 'asked'. Ask students to replace each instance of 'said' in the text with one of the following:

| | | | |
|---|---|---|---|
| responded | replied | suggested | demanded |
| ordered | begged | cautioned | whispered |
| muttered | snarled | hinted | chuckled |

Finally, ask students what they think are the advantages or disadvantages of 'colourful' reporting verbs. This activity can also be used with any piece of prose text which features excessive use of the word 'said' after speech.

## Narrative

An important element of many texts is **narrative**, which we all use when we tell a story. Consider the following examples: a news story, a personal anecdote, and a traditional nursery rhyme.

**Surprise book find**

A copy of William Shakespeare's First Folio, published in 1623, has been recently found by a librarian in France, sorting books for a forthcoming exhibition. It is unknown how long the volume may have been there. The book, discovered in a local library in Calais, is estimated to be worth several million pounds.

**Patio picnic**

I once had a cat called Timmy, who was a really good companion. One sunny afternoon I was relaxing in my garden, when I decided to get a cup of tea and a piece of cake. As soon as I had sat down and started to eat the cake, Timmy pushed his front paws into a bush and drew out a dead pigeon. He then sat next to me and while I ate my cake, he chewed on the pigeon. When I finished the cake, he put the remains of the pigeon back into the bush, and we both went indoors.

**Solomon Grundy**

Solomon Grundy
Born on a Monday
Named on Tuesday
Married on Wednesday
Fell ill on Thursday
Got worse on Friday
Died on Saturday
Buried on Sunday
That was the end of Solomon Grundy.

TEXTS 1.10–1.12 *Examples of non-literary narratives*

We are not suggesting that Texts 1.10–1.12 are literary works. The point is that the same patterns and devices can occur in literary and non-literary texts. Looking at short and often simple non-literary texts like these can help prepare learners for more complex texts.

Other examples of narrative can be found in jokes, ballads (both written and sung), pop-songs, and urban myths. The latter are typically oral tales, but they can also be found written down, or even appear as news stories and in political speeches. A common urban myth involves a car driver who gives a lift to a hitchhiker who suddenly vanishes into thin air. The driver subsequently discovers that they picked up the hitchhiker at a place where someone recently died.

**Try this** ☞ **Sharing different types of narrative**

Ask students to tell any jokes or urban myths they know in L1 or in English.
Ask them to bring in poems or songs in their L1 which have a clear narrative.

# 2 Approaches and techniques

## Overall approach

It goes without saying that the core aim of a language classroom is to teach and practise language. However, once we use literature in the language classroom, we need to think about why we are doing it, and what our approach to literature and its use in the classroom is.

Three approaches to this issue are often cited, and each has different implications for how you will deal with the works that you decide to include or that are on your prescribed syllabus.

The first approach sees literature as a body of knowledge and as content – for example, examining styles in literature, studying the history of English literature, dealing with the facts of authors' lives, etc. In this approach, literary texts are mostly taken from the literary **canon**, normally written before the middle of the 20th century, and are often long.

The second approach sees literature purely as language practice material, where the focus is primarily (or even exclusively) on the language used in the literary text, and incorporating practice tasks which activate language skills. In such cases, the texts are probably modern and are often short and there is little, if any, discussion of the text as literature.

A third approach sees literature as a stimulus for personal development, and uses activities which relate to students' personal experiences, thereby developing their imagination and emotions.

An additional classification of approaches to literature is outlined in the work of Louise Rosenblatt, who defined two ways of reading literature: **efferent reading** and **aesthetic reading**. By efferent reading, Rosenblatt means an approach which focuses on the public knowledge which a reader takes away from a text. This includes the **plot** of a novel, the characters in a play, and the literary devices such as use of rhyme, **metre** and **stanza** in poetry. It also includes the type of knowledge that is included in the first approach mentioned above. By aesthetic reading, Rosenblatt means the personal, private engagement of the reader with literature: the immersion in a novel which we find personally engaging; the feeling that the world outside has disappeared while we are watching a play; the sense of sympathy or empathy which we experience when reading a particularly apt poem. This is often seen as leading to the personal development mentioned in the third approach above.

Many teachers now adopt Rosenblatt's view of aesthetic reading as a major element of their use of literature, believing that it is important for learners to experience literature in a pleasurable, engrossing way. The activities in this book aim to make it easier for learners to do so. This does not mean that we ignore the first approach above, and to some extent there must always be some element of efferent reading. In order to express their feelings and thoughts about a text, learners (as all readers) have to be able to discuss plot, characters, or themes, and few, if any, classroom reading experiences can be wholly aesthetic. Information and facts about a work and an author often enhance learners' appreciation and understanding of the text.

Enjoyment and appreciation need to come first, however, with knowledge elements brought in to support this enjoyment and deepen existing understanding. Pedagogically, this means that this knowledge is often brought in at a late stage in the teaching cycle, after learners have already reacted to the text. Other elements are also important: as language teachers, we need to ensure that the literature we use also helps learners develop their language through exposure and meaningful practice, and from an educational point of view, engaging with literature contributes to learners' personal development.

It is important to note that the various approaches mentioned above can interact in ways which ensure that whichever facet of literature we decide to focus on, our teaching can incorporate a great deal of language practice in the form of fluency activities, discussion, vocabulary work, and of course exposure through reading. Even when focusing on the knowledge of facts about literature, it is possible to devise learner-centred tasks that will provide learners with plenty of practice.

## Starting with learners' experience

In the previous section we mentioned the importance of enjoying literature and experiencing it. There are a number of challenges to achieving this: learners may think of literature as remote from their own lives; they may not see themselves as readers of literature; they may resist material that the teacher brings to class. In some cases, literature may not be part of your syllabus and you may feel that you need to discuss its use with your class before bringing in a text to look at.

In this section we present a number of activities focusing on awareness-raising with learners, exploring their experience and their attitudes towards literature and its study. These activities are geared towards making learners aware that they actually experience a variety of literary works in their own lives, in preparation for introducing literature into the English language classroom. The activities also tap into their own L1 reading experience.

**Try this** ☞    **Find someone who**

This is a well-known speaking activity which gets students mingling with as many classmates as possible. Students can refer to things that they have read either in their L1 or English. First, give them a handout with the nine points listed below. Students then make questions from the points and ask classmates, for example, 'Do you like reading thrillers?' When they get a 'yes' answer, they write the student's name next to the point, and move on to another student. When everyone has a list with at least six names, move to a plenary discussion. One way of rounding up the activity is to ask for interesting stories that came up in the activity, or to elicit one or two examples from the whole class for each of the questions.

**Find someone who ...**

1  likes reading thrillers.
2  has never read any of the Harry Potter novels.
3  has read one work of fiction more than twice.
4  only reads a novel if they liked the film.
5  only watches films and would never read the novel.
6  is reading a book that you have never heard of.
7  is reading one of your favourite books.
8  has a favourite poem.
9  is part of a drama group and acts in plays.

✓ *Getting it right*

**Tailoring *Find someone who* to your students' needs**

You can construct your own statements for students, tailored to their language level or the specific circumstances in your country (e.g. by mentioning a local work of fiction). You can also use fewer questions if you want students to go beyond finding the answers and to discuss some of their views in pairs.

**Try this** ☞ **What makes you read**

This activity looks at reading as a social phenomenon, and encourages students to reflect on the way in which they make decisions about what to read: whether these decisions are individual, influenced by social media, by peers, etc. Once students have completed Table 2.1, ask them to consider the factors that influence their choice of reading, and the extent to which the decision to read a book is made on their own or influenced by others.

|  | Rarely | Sometimes | Often |
|---|---|---|---|
| I read books that I have seen my friends read. |  |  |  |
| I rely on suggestions from one or two specific people. |  |  |  |
| I get suggestions for what to read from online reviews. |  |  |  |
| I follow suggestions for what to read from one specific blog that I like. |  |  |  |
| I read books that I have seen mentioned in a number of places. |  |  |  |
| I only read what is compulsory in school. |  |  |  |
| I often read a book if I have seen a good film based on it. |  |  |  |
| I read books because their cover is visually attractive. |  |  |  |
| I buy books that are promoted by my local bookstore. |  |  |  |

TABLE 2.1 *What makes you read?*

**Why this works**

> **Getting students fully involved**
>
> These activities can be useful ice-breakers at the start of the academic year when students don't yet know each other well. The activities tap into students' own experiences, thus validating them. The 'Find someone who' activity is fluency-focused, making use of a range of possible question and answer structures. These activities also legitimize different genres and different approaches. The points to be discussed can be varied, depending on students' age, likely knowledge and interests, or level of English; in other words, you can adapt these activities to suit your learners. The 'What makes you read' activity allows students to express their prejudices without fear, and illustrates to them that all viewpoints are valid.

## Responding to literature

To ensure that literature is a pleasurable experience for learners, it is important to focus on how they respond to it, and on their own reactions. The most important questions a teacher can ask in the classroom are questions such as, 'Did you enjoy this?', 'What did you feel when you read this story?', 'Why did you feel this?' Such questions value and validate learners' responses, and open up the possibility of discussion.

✓ *Getting it right*

**Explaining likes and dislikes**

Remember that we don't all like the same works of literature, and we can't expect students to like everything. It is important to be open to this possibility and make this point to students. However, it is important is to develop students' ability to explain why they don't like a piece and what they don't like about it. Through explaining their likes and dislikes and discussing them with others, students learn to articulate their feelings and opinions, and of course gain useful fluency practice.

### Examining different reactions

One way to promote discussion is to provide students with a selection of 'ready-made' reactions to the poem or story you are studying. The best way of doing this is to ask colleagues and/or friends to read and react to them. Ask them also to explain why they react or feel the way they do. It's best if you do this by email, so that you have it in writing. After reading the poem/story, show students the different reactions, and ask them to comment on them.

If you do this on a handout, you can also work with students on phrases or words that signal reactions. This will help them learn how to verbalize their reactions as well as how to support their opinions.

The well-known poem *If* by Rudyard Kipling in Text 2.1 often provokes quite contrasting reactions from readers. The five responses appearing below Text 2.1 were written by different readers from a variety of educational backgrounds. Some reacted to the theme, some reacted to the rhythm, but no one remained indifferent. You can use these responses in a variety of ways:

- Ask students to choose the response they most identify with.
- Choose useful phrases from these responses and show students how they are used.
- Choose a variety of phrases and ask students to classify them into informal and formal ones (e.g. 'maximum punch'; 'the message really sinks in' as against 'a memorable poem'; 'ingrained in our cultural heritage', etc.).

---

**If**

If you can keep your head when all about you
    Are losing theirs and blaming it on you,
If you can trust yourself when all men doubt you,
    But make allowance for their doubting too;
If you can wait and not be tired by waiting,
    Or being lied about, don't deal in lies,
Or being hated, don't give way to hating,
    And yet don't look too good, nor talk too wise:

If you can dream—and not make dreams your master;
    If you can think—and not make thoughts your aim;
If you can meet with Triumph and Disaster
    And treat those two impostors just the same;
If you can bear to hear the truth you've spoken
    Twisted by knaves to make a trap for fools,
Or watch the things you gave your life to, broken,
    And stoop and build 'em up with worn-out tools:

If you can make one heap of all your winnings
    And risk it on one turn of pitch-and-toss,
And lose, and start again at your beginnings
    And never breathe a word about your loss;
If you can force your heart and nerve and sinew
    To serve your turn long after they are gone,
And so hold on when there is nothing in you
    Except the Will which says to them: 'Hold on!'

If you can talk with crowds and keep your virtue,
    Or walk with Kings—nor lose the common touch,
If neither foes nor loving friends can hurt you,
    If all men count with you, but none too much;
If you can fill the unforgiving minute
    With sixty seconds' worth of distance run,
Yours is the Earth and everything that's in it,
    And—which is more—you'll be a Man, my son!

---

TEXT 2.1     *If (1910) by Rudyard Kipling*

### Readers' reactions

1   I do like this poem, though mainly because of the way it reads, rather than the subject matter. The rhythm carries you forward, it's an easy read and carries a good sentiment. Though personally I prefer my poetry a little more obscure and less palatable, I think this poem is so ingrained in our cultural heritage it's hard not to feel stirred by it.

2  It's a great poem. It's as if it was written for me and about me – it's about how you get knocked down and manage to get up again.

3  Actually this is first time I've read it. So to me it is about being honest, able to mix with anyone on any level, not worrying about loss. Exactly as one should be! As I would hope my kids to be. Am not a poetry fan but liked this.

4  I love this poem. It feels strong the way he repeats key words in the first verse, to reiterate each quality. The rhyming makes it really easy to follow. I like the use of 'if' at the start of each line. Again it's repetitive so the message really sinks in. The poem is really uplifting and each time I read it I want to take on those qualities and be that kind of person.

5  *If* is an old familiar poem and as a reader I cannot entirely shrug off previous impressions of inspiration and power because the poem has old associations for me. I think it is best read out loud for maximum punch. It is of its time, thus outdated, so I do not take offence that the aspirations in the poem are for boys only. Sexist, assumptive, sentimental, inspirational and effective. Of course it is a load of idealistic rubbish, but it remains a memorable poem which, deserved or not, lurks at the edge of much of the nation's psyche.

**Try this** ☞ **You don't always have to like it!**

Choose a poem that is well written but that you may not particularly like yourself. Bring it to class and ask students to react. Then surprise them by giving your own view and discuss their response.

**Try this** ☞ **Examining critical reactions**

Choose three or four short reactions from critics or online reviews that refer to the text that you are studying. Try to find critical reactions that contradict each other, as these are likely to promote more discussion, and signal to the learners that it is possible to have very different views of the same text. (See page 40 for an example of this activity for the poem *Richard Cory*.)

## Sensitizing learners to key themes

We have discussed the ways in which we choose what to read. In the classroom, however, learners often do not choose: the teacher chooses for them. In some settings, the teacher has no choice either, and has to teach a text prescribed by the curriculum. In such cases, it is a good idea to plan a lesson or series of lessons to arouse learners' interest and connect the topic to their lives and experiences.

Part of the potency of literary texts is that they often deal with the key issues of human life: birth, love and marriage, death. Because these are issues that we have all experienced, directly or indirectly, literary texts are more than just the words on the page. Even younger people will have experience and opinions about most, if not all, of these issues. Each reader brings to a text their own experiences and their own imagination, so that each person, in a sense, 'writes' their own text. That text then incorporates the reader's own reactions and their personal resonances, as we saw in the various reactions to the poem *If*.

Clearly, these resonances have to be anchored to reality and to the text. This is where the teacher comes in, providing essential support and guidance. The following activities are designed to activate learners' knowledge, show them how to relate texts to their own lives, and to help them realize that they have the freedom to bring in their own life experiences and gain ownership of the text. These activities can be done before a detailed analysis of the text, but also at the end of the teaching cycle.

## Theme 1: Birth and early life

Many autobiographies, biographies, and autobiographical novels begin with the birth and early life of the main character. Examples include Boswell's *Life of Johnson* (1791), Charles Dickens' novel *David Copperfield* (1850), Frank McCourt's *Angela's Ashes* (1996), and JG Ballard's *Miracles of Life* (2008). This is a fruitful area to explore, as everyone has personal experience to contribute to discussion. In the activities below we refer to *Robinson Crusoe* (1709) by Daniel Defoe, a novel which was long thought to be an account of the real-life experiences of its author. The methodology we suggest here could be used with any other text that you plan to spend some time on.

### Short verbal introduction

Give a short introduction to the book that you wish to focus on. For example, for the novel we are considering:
'Robinson Crusoe *is the fictitious account of a shipwrecked sailor's adventures alone on a desert island. It was written by Daniel Defoe and first published in 1709.*'
Note that this introduction is very short, and in effect, learners enter the novel 'at the deep end'.

### Brainstorming and mind-mapping

Take some of the key concepts in the works you plan to study and ask students, in groups, to suggest words and ideas that relate to these concepts. These words and ideas can first be listed, and then organized into mind-maps. Afterwards, you can indicate or highlight the words and ideas that will turn out to be most important. For *Robinson Crusoe*, the following are some of the key concepts:
- Choosing a career, including going against parental wishes
- Losing contact with one's family
- Being shipwrecked
- Trying to survive alone on a desert island.

Figure 2.1 is a mind-map generated for *Robinson Crusoe*. Note how the different associations to the central theme – surviving on a desert island – are organized into different groups.

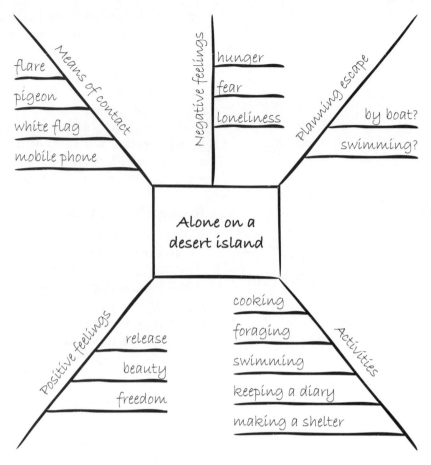

FIGURE 2.1    *Mind-map for Robinson Crusoe*

### Opening paragraph or page

The opening sentence, paragraph, or page usually sets the scene for what is to follow. Sometimes you will want to read through the first pages without constructing too many associated activities in order to get learners interested in the book. In other cases, you may wish to make sure that learners identify key elements in the novel from the very beginning.

One way of doing this is to work with the vocabulary of the text. First, identify key vocabulary from the opening paragraphs, i.e. words that are important in the early stages of the novel (or even throughout). These may be difficult words, which it will be necessary for students to understand. However, do not present all the difficult words: focus on those that most need to be understood. Then give the first paragraphs to students with the text gapped, but with the missing words jumbled beneath the text, and ask them to fill the gaps. (Note that by supplying the words they choose from, we make this into a teaching activity; if we presented it as a traditional gapped text, this would become a testing activity.)

**Opening of Robinson Crusoe**

I was born in the year 1632, in the city of York, of a good family, though not of that country, my father being a foreigner of Bremen, who settled first at Hull. He got a good estate by merchandise and, leaving off his trade, lived afterwards at York, from whence he had married my [1]_____, whose relations were named Robinson, a very good family in that country, and from whom I was called Robinson Kreutznaer; but by the usual corruption of [2]_____ in England we are now called, nay, we call ourselves, and write our name, Crusoe, and so my companions always called me.

I had two elder [3]_____, one of which was lieutenant-colonel to an English regiment of foot in Flanders, formerly commanded by the famous Colonel Lockhart, and was killed at the [4]_____ near Dunkirk against the Spaniards; what became of my second brother I never [5]_____, any more than my father and mother did know what was become of me.

Being the third [6]_____ of the family, and not bred to any trade, my head began to be filled very early with [7]_____ thoughts. My father, who was very ancient, had given me a competent share of learning, as far as house-education and a country free-school generally goes, and designed me for the law; but I would be [8]_____ with nothing but going to sea and my [9]_____ to this led me so strongly against the will, nay, [10]_____, of my father, and against all the entreaties and persuasions of my mother and other friends, that there seemed to be something fatal in that propension of nature tending directly to the life of misery which was to befall me.

| battle | mother | words | commands | son |
|--------|--------|-------|----------|-----|
| knew | rambling | brothers | inclination | satisfied |

**Answers:** 1 mother, 2 words, 3 brothers, 4 battle, 5 knew, 6 son, 7 rambling, 8 satisfied, 9 inclination, 10 commands

TEXT 2.2    *Gap-fill version of opening of* Robinson Crusoe *(1709) by Daniel Defoe*

After this activity, discuss the extract with students. The questions below relate to the main points of the paragraph.

**Questions**

1 The male members of the Crusoe family have all travelled. Underline or list the place names which are mentioned in Paragraphs 1 and 2. Can you locate them on a map?

2 In Paragraph 2, we learn that Robinson Crusoe's family has broken up. What has happened to his brothers? What does he hint at in the last line of Paragraph 2?

3 In Paragraph 3, Robinson Crusoe describes his education, character and his plans for a career. What impression do you have of him? (Key words/ phrases: 'rambling and satisfied with nothing'.)

4 What might be hinted at in the word 'misery' in the final sentence of the extract?

5 Would you like to go on reading about Robinson Crusoe? What would/ wouldn't make you want to read on? What else would you like to learn about in the novel?

### Who is the narrator?

As mentioned above, *Robinson Crusoe* was long thought to be a true story; the use of the first person for the narrative was surely an important trigger for this mistaken view, and a clever choice on the part of the author. Now ask students to rewrite the beginning of *Robinson Crusoe* in the third person, using he. One of the benefits of this is that learners will see how the narrative becomes less immediate and, in effect, less convincing.

## Theme 2: Love and marriage

Many comedies and comic novels deal with the themes of love and marriage: all Shakespeare's comedies, for example; Oscar Wilde's *The Importance of Being Earnest*; the novels of Jane Austen and their modern offshoots (e.g. *Bridget Jones's Diary* by Helen Fielding). The following activities provide ways of introducing these themes before leading into whichever play or novel you are studying.

Learners can be asked to discuss or work through some of the activities, using their own experience and ideas as well as those of their families and friends. An important element is for learners to reflect on possible differences between the present and the past, since many of the literary works they will be studying in both their L1 and English were written in a previous century. (Obviously, you also need to be careful of any sensitive or cultural issues within a particular group.)

**Try this** ☞  **Historical overview on finding a romantic partner**

Ask students to complete Table 2.2, which focuses on the ways in which people find partners.

|  | My generation | My grandparents' generation | Previous generations |
|---|---|---|---|
| 1  At school/college/ university |  |  |  |
| 2  At work |  |  |  |
| 3  Through a dating agency |  |  |  |
| 4  Through parents or family |  |  |  |
| 5  At a club or other social venue |  |  |  |
| 6  By other means |  |  |  |

TABLE 2.2   *Finding a romantic partner*

**Try this** ☞    **Unusual ways to find a partner**

Ask students to describe an unusual way that a couple they know became partners.

**Try this** ☞    **What's important in a partner?**

Ask students to consider the attributes in Table 2.3 and to mark the ones that they think are important to most people. Ask them if they can think of any more. Can they rank them? Many people think that men and women differ in what they look for in a partner – do they agree? The issues involved were particularly important in the past, for example in the novels of Jane Austen and Charles Dickens, and so we need to be aware of them when tackling older works of literature.

| | What men look for in a partner | What women look for in a partner | What was important in the past | What is important now |
|---|---|---|---|---|
| Wealth | | | | |
| Sense of humour | | | | |
| Physical attractiveness | | | | |
| Tolerance and ability to compromise | | | | |
| Attitude to spending money | | | | |
| Practical skills (e.g. cooking, DIY) | | | | |
| Sense of fun | | | | |
| Intelligence | | | | |
| Higher social class | | | | |
| Youth | | | | |

TABLE 2.3    *Important qualities in a partner*

**Try this** ☞    **Famous weddings**

Use photos of famous weddings to initiate a discussion of weddings and marriage. Such examples help learners to examine the concept of marriage, positioning it historically and within current social customs. You could also use photos and covers of popular magazines, which often have more 'sensational' wedding photos of celebrities, raising the question of why readers are so interested in such information. Interestingly, this latter option may also give rise to discussion related to weddings between couples who have been previously married, same-sex couples, or those who already have children. (You will need to be careful of any sensitive or cultural issues within a particular group.)

## More techniques to use with texts

In this section we provide examples for a number of techniques that can be used effectively with a variety of texts. Many of them fall into the category of textual intervention, in which learners are asked to intervene in the text and change it in some way, and then examine the effect that these changes have.

### Gapping words or sentences

Many poems lend themselves to taking words out and asking learners to work creatively to supply the missing words or lines. We have shown the way gapping words can bring out themes in the example from *Robinson Crusoe*. Here we show a different example, in which one line has been taken out of a poem.

Present Text 2.3 to the class, telling them that the last line in the poem is missing and that their task is to write a last line in pairs or groups of three. It's best if you read the poem aloud to the class at least once or twice, and then clarify any language points that you think learners may not be able to work out for themselves.

---

**Richard Cory**

Whenever Richard Cory went down town,
We people on the pavement looked at him:
He was a gentleman from sole to crown,
Clean favored, and imperially slim.

And he was always quietly arrayed,
And he was always human when he talked,
But still he fluttered pulses when he said,
'Good morning', and he glittered when he walked.

And he was rich – yes, richer than a king –
And admirably schooled in every grace:
In fine, we thought that he was everything
To make us wish that we were in his place.

So on we worked, and waited for the light,
And went without the meat, and cursed the bread;
And Richard Cory, one calm summer night,

---

TEXT 2.3    Richard Cory *(1897) by Edward Arlington Robinson*

Once most pairs have a last line, ask them to write their completions on the board, compare them, and discuss the differences. Then read the poem from the beginning and supply the actual last line: 'Went home and put a bullet through his head'. (You should obviously be sensitive since the subject of suicide is not easy to raise or discuss in some classroom contexts.)

This task requires learners to activate their knowledge about the formal aspects of poetry (e.g. knowledge of rhyme scheme or metre) and their knowledge of the way literature works thematically (e.g. how writers build up someone who is perfect only to bring them down at the end). They may often also bring in knowledge of life, such as the fact that no one is perfect; everyone has a flaw of some type or another.

**✓ Getting it right**

**Gapping poems**

Make sure that the words or sentences you gap are important to the meaning of the poem, and that thinking about them will make learners reflect on the main themes of the poem (see the activity using Oscar Wilde's *Symphony in Yellow* in Chapter 5). One poem where this works well is Gerald England's *To M.M.*, where you can gap the words that describe the two **protagonists** in the poem. You could also use this type of activity with the poem *No!* by Thomas Hood on page 45.

## Walkabout

The walkabout is a simple technique in which you put texts up on the wall of the classroom. Students walk about the room and read the different texts. They then stand next to the text that they prefer, and discuss the reasons for their choice in small groups. Each group then reports back in a whole-class discussion. Alternatively, you can ask two or three students to comment individually on what they have read.

This is a good way to get students out of their seats and moving, and therefore suitable for times when energy levels in the classrooms are low (e.g. after lunch). Because the groups are mixed according to their choice of text, this means students also get to talk to classmates they might not often talk to.

**Try this ☞**  **Walkabout with poems by one poet**

Do a walkabout with short poems by one poet: for example, choose four or five poems by Emily Dickinson, whose poetry is very short and often memorable. This means that students will read and experience several poems in a short space of time.

**Try this ☞**  **Walkabout focused on one topic**

Do a walkabout using poems about the same topic: for example, poems on school and schooling, such as Brian Patten's *The Minister for Exams*, Wendy Cope's *Team Spirit*, Charles Causley's *Timothy Winters*, or Vernon Scannell's *Ageing Headmaster*.

**Try this ☞**  **Walkabout with critics' reviews**

Find a few contrasting opinions of the text that you are using and put them up on the walls. Below are three critical views which can be used if you are teaching *Richard Cory* by Edward Arlington Robinson.

### Critical views

*Richard Cory*, so widely known among Robinson's short poems because it is clear in style and thought, has a surprise ending, withholding until the final line the contrast between the outward material success and the hidden despair, between the calm summer night and the desperate deed.

(ADAPTED FROM EMERY NEFF, *EDWIN ARLINGTON ROBINSON*)

... not only do we get the essence of poetry in these poems, we get drama. In four words, 'one calm summer night', the poet sets a background for the tragedy which brings the bullet shot crashing across our ear-drums with the shock of an earthquake.

(ADAPTED FROM AMY LOWELL, *TENDENCIES IN MODERN AMERICAN POETRY*)

In *Richard Cory* ... we have a superficially neat portrait of the elegant man of mystery; the poem builds up deliberately to a very cheap surprise ending; but all surprise endings are cheap in poetry, for poetry is written to be read not once but many times.

(ADAPTED FROM YVOR WINTERS, *EDWIN ARLINGTON ROBINSON*, NORFOLK)

 *Getting it right*

**Walkabout texts**

The texts for a walkabout activity need to be short, so that everyone can read them all and have enough time for discussion in groups. If you have chosen the texts, make sure that they are printed in a large font so that three or more students can read them easily at the same time. You can also do a walkabout with students' own texts, in which case they will be in smaller print or even handwriting. This is acceptable as long as they are aware that not everyone will be able to read everything. It is, in fact, possible to do a walkabout in any kind of room, including an auditorium with fixed seats.

 *Getting it right*

**Choosing critics' views**

It is now quite easy to find collections of critics' views online. There is a website with critical views of *Richard Cory* on page 139. It is important to choose contrasting views, so that at least one or two of the critics point out problems with the text you are studying, as for example, the quote by Yvor Winters.

## Creating different versions of a text

We may think of literary texts as fixed, unchanging, and unchangeable. In fact, they can be the subject of many changes: in the successive drafts produced by the author, or as the result of editing by someone else (for example, Ezra Pound's drastic editing of TS Eliot's poem *The Waste Land* or the heavy cuts and changes made to Raymond Carver's short stories by his editor, Gordon Lish). Exploring alternative versions of texts is a fruitful way for learners to understand how texts achieve their effects. The techniques below require learners to change one or two significant elements in a text, noting and making any further necessary changes. We presented one example of this, changing the narrator of *Robinson Crusoe* (Text 2.2).

**Try this** ☞ **Seeing another character's point of view**

This activity involves sensitivity to the role of the narrator and what they choose to tell or not tell the reader. Especially with a first-person narrator, this involves understanding the limitations of the narrator and examining their reliability. This could entail thinking of events that are not mentioned in the story, or presenting events that are described, but from a different point of view. We provide some examples in Chapter 4.

**Try this** ☞ **Bringing a story up to the present day**

One way of intervening with a text is bringing it up to the present day. For example, in Dorothy Parker's *A Telephone Call*, students could imagine what would change (e.g. the narrator would probably be switching from her mobile phone to her email account to her Facebook page) and what would stay the same (e.g. the deep anxiety about a man calling or not calling). A recent example is Will Self's *Dorian: An Imitation*, an updating of Oscar Wilde's *The Picture of Dorian Gray*, in which the picture in the attic has become a video installation which literally and physically disintegrates with time.

**Try this** ☞ **Changing the identity of the main character**

An effective way of understanding what the author is doing, and how they are achieving their effects, is to imagine that the work is about a different protagonist. For example, asking students to change the gender of the main protagonist entails examining gender roles and gender stereotypes and the way they are represented in the text they are looking at. One recent example is a re-writing of the beginning of Virginia Woolf's *Mrs Dalloway* as 'Mr Dalloway': this involves understanding gender roles in the first quarter of the 20th century. Another example would be to imagine how Oscar Wilde's *The Picture of Dorian Gray* would work with a female protagonist. How would Dorothy Parker's short story *The Standard of Living* develop if the two women looking in a shop window were two male office workers on their lunch break?

## In at the deep end

In many of the activities in this book, we suggest ways of introducing learners to the work that you are teaching. However, in some cases, you can simply introduce a poem, a short story, or even the beginning of a novel to learners with no linguistic or background preparation, and ask them to read or react. This is, after all, the way in which we normally read literature – although we may know something about the author or text we are about to read (through having read either a review or the blurb on the back cover), often the beginning of a book is quite different from what we know about it and expect.

Good poems for this are short, lyrical poems, for example, Eavan Boland's *This Moment* and the poems of Emily Dickinson. The beginnings of John Steinbeck's *Of Mice and Men* and of Beverley Naidoo's *The Other Side of Truth* also lend themselves to reading with no preparation. (See pages 95–96 for a discussion of these two openings.)

**Try this** ☞    **Comments in the margin**

Provide the extract on a handout but leave plenty of space around it and ask students to write their reactions in the margin. Tell them that they will not be forced to discuss their reactions; that way they will feel free to write whatever they want. You can discuss your own reactions, or ask for a few volunteers to describe theirs, but make sure that you keep your promise not to force people to talk about their reactions. This validates their feelings and helps them to develop an authentic reaction and move towards experiential, aesthetic reading of texts.

**Try this** ☞    **Poem in every lesson**

One way of introducing your classes to a large variety of poems is to present them with one short poem every lesson, without going into a long discussion of any of them. Write the poem beforehand on the board, project it as your initial slide, or have a large printout of it fixed to the wall or board. After students have noticed the poem, spend no more than a couple of minutes reading it and maybe say a word or two about it. Good sources of short poems for this are by the Liverpool Poets (Roger McGough, Brian Patten, and Adrian Henri, as well as Adrian Mitchell); poems by Robert Frost or e e cummings; or children's poems by Michael Rosen or Charles Causley. Limericks also work well. The series of anthologies *Poems on the Underground* is a particularly good source since the poems in this series have to be short enough to fit a shallow poster size on London underground trains.

**Why this works** ⮕

> **The importance of variety**
>
> By introducing learners to a large variety of poems and spending only a short time on them, you are demystifying poetry – making it part of the life of the classroom and the life of learners. By having a large number of poems, you are also illustrating the variety of poetry and the fact that it deals with many themes and can be serious or humorous. You are showing learners that it is not always necessary to have a 'deep' discussion of a poem – sometimes it's enough to simply experience it, enjoy it, and move on.

## Working with sayings and proverbs

Presenting the class with a list of sayings can be a good pre-reading exercise, sensitizing them to the theme. Alternatively, you can present a list of proverbs and sayings after you have worked on a play or novel, and ask learners to choose the ones that are closest in point of view to the text you have studied.

**Try this** ☞    **Sayings about money**

This list can be used when teaching *The Merchant of Venice*, O Henry's short story *Mammon and the Archer*, Dorothy Parker's *The Standard of Living*, and many other texts. Ask students how many they know and to what extent they agree with them.

1 All that glitters is not gold.
2 If a man is a miser, he will certainly have a prodigal son.
3 Much coin, much care.
4 When we have gold, we are in fear. When we have none, we are in danger.
5 A rich man can do nothing wrong.
6 A heavy purse makes a light heart.

*Getting it right*

**Finding quotes online**

There are many websites with lists of sayings, proverbs, and famous quotes on a large number of topics. You can enter a general topic (e.g. 'proverbs about love') or you could narrow your search by using more specific terms (e.g. 'proverbs about love at first sight'). You can then decide whether you want to focus only on famous sayings originally in English or whether you also want to choose famous sayings translated from other languages into English.

**Why this works**

**Sayings and proverbs as everyday poetry**

Sayings and proverbs are in themselves examples of how ideas are often expressed in a literary or poetic way: they often employ devices such as alliteration, parallelism, or a regular metre. Because there are many sayings for almost any theme that you might deal with in class, this is an easy activity to construct. It introduces learners to elements of English-speaking cultures and serves as a springboard for fluency-oriented activities.

## Reading aloud

Reading aloud has a different function in each of the genres that you may use in the classroom. Poetry and plays are quite clearly meant to be performed in a spoken mode – either read aloud or acted. It is important that learners should hear the poems they are studying and not just read them, and it is just as important that they hear a play being acted (or even better, see a performance). With prose, the situation is different. It is sometimes possible to read a whole short story aloud, especially if it is only two or three pages long. On the other hand, it is probably not a good idea to read a whole novel to the class. Reading aloud long passages from a text takes a great deal of time, and increases the dependency of learners on the teacher. However, if the teacher reads aloud selected passages from time to time, this has a number of advantages for teachers and learners:

- It strengthens the links between the written form and the spoken form. This is particularly useful for learners who may be dyslexic. It can help learners identify words which they can recognize by sound but can't identify by sight.
- Because the teacher is reading aloud, learners are prevented from stopping for every unknown word: this helps them practise the all-important skill of ignoring what they do not understand and going along with what they can understand, thus contributing to fluent reading.
- The teacher's intonation and gestures can often clarify points which would otherwise escape them, thus enhancing comprehension of the text. For example, a teacher can highlight positive or negative connotations of words through stress and intonation. Intonation and gestures can also contribute to the understanding of humorous texts.
- If learners are not following the text in their copies, and are listening to the teacher reading aloud, the teacher can substitute difficult words for words that they know learners will understand.

Some teachers feel uncomfortable reading aloud to their classes, because they think that this requires additional skills which they do not possess. In fact, it is possible for every teacher to learn how to read aloud to the class, and we make a few suggestions for how to do this below. If you still feel uncomfortable reading aloud, it's worth remembering that many books have an audiobook version, and it can be equally beneficial for learners to listen to it in this way. It also has the benefit of introducing an additional voice and accent into the classroom.

In some countries, there is a tradition of asking learners to read a passage of text aloud in class. We said above that some teachers think that reading aloud requires special skill, and this point would be even more relevant when learners are asked to do it. Having said this, there are times when it is possible for this to become a useful learning activity – for example, if the teacher makes sure that learners are given sufficient time and support to prepare a specific passage for reading aloud and it becomes a form of dramatization.

✓ *Getting it right*

**Reading aloud**

If you read aloud to your class, make sure that you practise reading the passage beforehand. You should know how to pronounce all the words in the text, and have a clear idea of where to pause during the reading, which words you are going to stress, etc. Practise reading in chunks, pausing between them, rather than at a pace that is uniformly slow. Make sure that your intonation varies and that you modulate your voice during the reading. While you read, hold the book – or the page – at a convenient distance and height so that you can read and watch the class at the same time. If you are reading from a handout rather than a book, print out the text in a large font so that you can read it comfortably. Making eye contact with students while you read aloud will make them feel part of the process. Allow students to follow in their copies of the book if they want to.

Try this ☞

**Recording yourself**

Record yourself reading the text aloud and then play the recording to students. This reduces the stress of doing a 'live' performance.

## Group performance of poems

In this technique, groups of learners are given a poem. Each group gets about 20 minutes to construct their reading before performing it to the class. This gives them time to read the poem, understand it, look words up in the dictionary for meaning and pronunciation, and decide on the format of the reading. It works well with poems where there are different protagonists, where there are two or more alternating moods, or where there is a refrain, a regular repetition of phrases (see Text 2.4 or Text 5.1 in Chapter 5).

## Jumbling sentences

This is a classic technique which is often used to help learners understand the structure of paragraphs. When used in the literature classroom, it helps them appreciate the way in which writers achieve their effects.

Text 2.4 lends itself well to a jumbled sentences technique: some of the connections are quite obvious because of the rhyme; other aspects of the order could be discussed (students may wish to put the word 'November' at the beginning, for example, and you could compare the effect of that). Another poem that lends itself to a jumbled sentences technique is *Lonely*

*Hearts* by Wendy Cope, partly because of its form, which includes a large number of repeated lines.

The best way of doing this is to type up the poem in a large font, print enough copies of the poem for each group of students, and cut up the lines. Students then have a physical copy of the poem which they can rearrange.

**Why this works** ▐▐▐▶

> **Learners' creative involvement**
>
> In many of the techniques above, learners are asked to create their own version of a poem or a story before being introduced to the original text that sparked off the activity. Experience tells us that learners like this type of activity because it gets them involved creatively and because thinking about this makes them curious about what the original writer wrote.

---

**No!**

No sun – no moon!
No morn – no noon!
No dawn – no dusk – no proper time of day –
No sky – no earthly view –
No distance looking blue –
No road – no street – no 't'other side this way' –
No end to any Row –
No indications where the Crescents go –
No top to any steeple –
No recognitions of familiar people –
No courtesies for showing 'em –
No knowing 'em!
No travelling at all – no locomotion –
No inkling of the way – no notion –
'No go' by land or ocean –
No mail – no post –
No news from any foreign coast –
No Park, no Ring, no afternoon gentility –
No company – no nobility –
No warmth, no cheerfulness, no healthful ease,
No comfortable feel in any member –
No shade, no shine, no butterflies, no bees,
No fruits, no flowers, no leaves, no birds –
November!

---

TEXT 2.4   No! *(1844) by Thomas Hood*

 *Getting it right*

> **Doable activities**
>
> In all the techniques above, it is important to ensure that the activity is doable by the students. For example, with the poem *Richard Cory*, almost all students realize that the ending can't be a good one, and most endings that students provide involve Richard Cory's death. Gerald England's poem, *To M.M.*, very clearly illustrates the progression of a relationship, and students are quick to realize this, which then helps them supply the missing words.

# Rounding up a series of lessons

The activities in this section highlight the need to make learners conscious of what they have done – either in a series of lessons or throughout the year – and present their reflections to the class in a concrete form.

**Try this** ☞    **Desert island discs**

One way of reviewing and revising the work of a year or term is to ask students to choose the three or four texts that they liked most and connect them to their own lives. This can copy the format of *Desert Island Discs*, a popular British radio programme in which a celebrity selects the eight musical tracks they would take to a desert island with them. (It is interesting to note that on this hypothetical island, all the celebrities are automatically given the Bible and the complete works of Shakespeare.)

**Try this** ☞    **Characters' lives as a road**

The road is a common metaphor for life and life's journey. Two well-known literary examples are the beginning of Dante's *Divine Comedy* and Robert Frost's *The Road Not Taken*. A useful exercise to sum up a story or novel is to ask students to think of the characters' lives and imagine the kind of road that they have taken. In Chapter 4, we discuss Susan Hill's story *How Soon Can I Leave?* in which the two main characters take very different paths through life. Asking students to draw these could result in a diagram such as Figure 2.2.

Learners could explain that Miss Roscommon's road is direct, uncomplicated, wide – or, at least, that is the way she sees it. Miss Bartlett's road is convoluted; maybe her life is best represented as different roads and side-roads clustering together, none clearly going anywhere. Either give this diagram to students and discuss it with them, or ask them to draw a pictorial representation themselves, show their classmates, and discuss it.

Preliminary language work could include eliciting and teaching different vocabulary connected to roads: 'highway', 'alley', 'lane', 'street', 'way', 'avenue', 'drive', 'cul-de-sac', 'dead end', etc. These could be categorized according to width, length, or importance. There are also collocations which have common resonances, for example, 'the straight and narrow' (the narrow path of virtue); 'the broad highway'.

**Try this** ☞    **Characters' lives as a tree**

A variation on the previous exercise is to think of the characters' lives as a tree: a common metaphor is 'the tree of life'; 'the family tree' is a common expression in many languages. Students can think of which tree the characters are, what the roots are like, how thick the trunk is, how numerous the branches are, etc.

ROADS IN LIFE

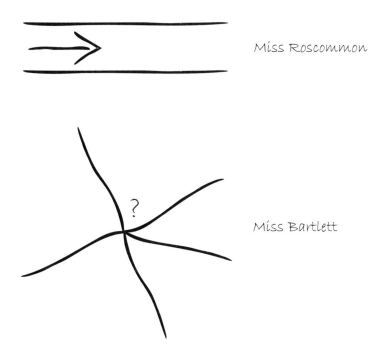

FIGURE 2.2    *Roads for the main characters in* How Soon Can I leave?

**Why this works** ▐▐▐➡

> **Engaging learners through tasks**
>
> The most important element in the approach above is the attempt to
> provide learners with activities that create engagement with literature. In
> most cases, their interaction with the literature is structured through an
> activity. For example, rather than ask learners to discuss what they do/don't
> like reading, they are asked to work with a focused handout and interview
> their classmates about their favourite genres. This structures the discussion
> and also provides tangible evidence that learners have done the work. The
> same is true of the walkabout procedure: it is easy to see which learners
> are reading the poems on the wall. It is also easy to see which learners have
> made a decision and who is wavering – making it possible for the teacher
> to intervene. In the same way, asking learners to draw diagrams or maps, to
> rearrange poems that are jumbled, and to produce a new version all have
> elements of task-based learning.

# 3   What readers bring to a text

## Types of knowledge

All communication builds on the assumption that there is shared knowledge between the people communicating. At the very basic level, there is shared knowledge of the language: its vocabulary, grammar, discourse conventions, and sociolinguistic conventions. Equally important is knowledge of the world: the way people interact, the formulaic ways in which interactions take place and the way interactions vary in different settings. Another important type of knowledge is factual knowledge, for example, history, geography, politics, etc.

Different words are used for our personal store of knowledge, but the one that is probably best known is *schema* (plural: *schemata*). According to schema theory, knowledge is organized in our minds in structures which facilitate its retrieval as well as its storage. Shared knowledge means that we can interpret utterances that are not totally explicit. So if a speaker says, 'I went to that new restaurant. It was excellent, but I was shocked when the bill arrived', a listener will understand that the speaker was shocked because the meal was expensive, rather than because they got a bill. This understanding is not only linguistic: it builds on an understanding that at a restaurant you have to pay for your food, that you have expectations of the size of a bill, etc. The restaurant schema is one of the best known examples: we all know what happens in restaurants in our own culture (though this may be different in other cultures).

Shared knowledge also comes into play when we are reading literature. For example, a famous short story by WS Maugham, *The Luncheon*, depends on the fact that in Western-style meals there is a series of courses, served one after the other. The story is about a young man taking an older woman to lunch. He has very little money, but she keeps choosing expensive items. The tension increases each time she chooses a new course: Will the young man be able to pay? To appreciate it, you need the basic knowledge that at a restaurant, food is paid for at the end of the meal; you also have to imagine a world where payment is only in cash, rather than on credit. Another example can be seen in the extract from Oscar Wilde's *The Importance of Being Earnest* (see Chapters 1 and 7), where part of the humour is rooted in the different views of what constitutes a 'proper' marriage proposal.

There are other types of knowledge that appear in many literary works – cultural knowledge, historical knowledge and intertextual knowledge. One example of cultural knowledge is the issue of names and their cultural connotations which comes up in *The Importance of Being Earnest*. Names also have historical and etymological connotations, as shown in the choice of name for the protagonist in the poem *Richard Cory* by Edwin Arlington Robinson (see Chapter 2). Both the first name and the second name have connections with power, influence, and riches. The name Richard, apart from its clear sound connections with the word 'rich', actually comes from an Old Germanic word which means 'a powerful warrior'. If we think of one of the most famous Richards in history – Richard the Lionheart, or Richard Coeur de Lion – the surname 'Cory' also takes on an additional meaning. All of this information is interesting and adds to our appreciation of the poet's art but it is not essential to an understanding of the poem or to an appreciation of its main points.

In most literary works, the writer makes quite a lot of assumptions about what knowledge the reader brings to the text. There are often several examples of **intertextual reference**. In some cases, you may be worried that you don't know 'everything' about the piece that you are studying and all its references. In fact, very few readers do know 'everything'; it is still possible to appreciate a text despite this.

In this respect, it is interesting to see what editors of classical works decide to gloss for the reader. For example, in EM Forster's *A Room with a View*, the Reverend Beebe recalls a time when Lucy, the heroine, played a piece by Beethoven. He had wondered whether she would play *Adelaide* or the march from *The Ruins of Athens*, but she actually played the first movement of the piano sonata Opus 111. The Penguin edition of the novel explains that the first items are 'popular songs based on Beethoven'. It does not explain that Opus 111 is Beethoven's last piano sonata; that it is not one of Beethoven's 'greatest hits', but amongst musicians is considered one of his greatest masterpieces; that the second movement (which Lucy did not play, to the Reverend Beebe's great relief) is a particular challenge to play – and to listen to. Lucy's choice says much about her – something which the reader not familiar with the pieces mentioned will not know – and something which in fact the editor of the Penguin edition tells us only partially. Does it matter? To the literature specialist it might; to the reader and to a teacher it does not: what is important to take from this example is that there is no perfect knowledge of all the meanings intended by a writer, and that it is possible to understand much with only a partial understanding of these meanings.

## Background knowledge as an integrated task

A good example of a text which builds on previous knowledge is Wilfred Owen's poem, *The Parable of the Old Man and the Young*. We use it as an example of the way in which using background knowledge – in this case, intertextual knowledge – can be turned into a task.

> **The Parable of the Old Man and the Young**
>
> So Abram rose, and clave the wood, and went,
> And took the fire with him, and a knife.
> And as they sojourned both of them together,
> Isaac the first-born spake and said, My Father,
> Behold the preparations, fire and iron,
> But where the lamb for this burnt-offering?
> Then Abram bound the youth with belts and straps,
> And builded parapets and trenches there,
> And stretchèd forth the knife to slay his son.
> When lo! an Angel called him out of heaven,
> Saying, Lay not thy hand upon the lad,
> Neither do anything to him, thy son.
> Behold! Caught in a thicket by its horns,
> A Ram. Offer the Ram of Pride instead.
>
> But the old man would not so, but slew his son,
> And half the seed of Europe, one by one.

TEXT 3.1     The Parable of the Old Man and the Young *(1920) by Wilfred Owen*

The poem requires knowledge of various pieces of background information, but knowledge of the biblical story of Abraham and Isaac is essential for understanding. Without knowing the story, the way in which the poem shatters the expectation that Abraham will spare his son will not have an effect on the reader. However, it isn't essential for learners to know that Owen is referring to World War I: we have taught this poem in classes where the learners assumed that the final couplet refers to World War II, and the impact of the poem was just as strong. Other pieces of information – for example, that Owen was killed on 4th November 1918, only a week before the Armistice, or that the poem was used by Benjamin Britten in his *War Requiem* – may contribute to an appreciation of the poem and its place in British cultural life and to an understanding of the life of the poet, but are still not essential to understanding the poem itself.

How would we teach this background knowledge to learners? A traditional approach would be for the teacher to tell learners the Biblical story of Abraham and Isaac, and then read the poem with them. A different approach, and probably a more effective one, is to ask learners to research the story themselves, and report back in a subsequent lesson before reading the poem. This turns finding out about the story into a task for the learners. Yet another way is to present the story of Abraham and Isaac to learners, and to ask them to compare the original story with the poem. (For the original story, see the additional resources on our accompanying website: www.oup.com/elt/teacher/itc)

What emerges from such a comparison is that Owen didn't just use the Biblical narrative as a basis for the action in his poem, but used very specific words and phrases from the Old Testament to actually construct it, sometimes making only minimal changes. Examples are 'rose', 'clave the wood', 'stretched forth his hand' in the narration; Isaac's question in the biblical story ('but where is the lamb for a burnt offering?'), which becomes, 'But where the lamb for this burnt-offering?' in the poem; the angel's words, 'Lay not thy hand upon the lad'. Clearly, Owen knew the story extremely well and probably had a copy of the Old Testament to hand as he wrote the poem. Learners can be asked to comment on the words that Owen added (e.g. 'trenches', a very potent word in the context of WWI – again, a piece of background knowledge which learners may or may not have); the words he omitted; or any other changes that he made. Some of this may require specialized knowledge, for example, the use of the name Abram instead of Abraham (Abram was his original name; in the Old Testament story, the letter 'h' was added when Abraham committed to monotheism; its lack suggests a pagan state of mind). The important point is that learners play an active role in acquiring this background knowledge.

**Why this works** ▶

### Integrating tasks into the lesson

This example illustrates a number of principles. Firstly, background knowledge here is provided as an integral part of the lesson: this knowledge is essential and is integrated into the lesson rather than as an additional extra. Secondly, this is an additional illustration of our general approach: giving learners responsibility for their learning and enabling them to take ownership of it in the form of a task.

✓ *Getting it right*

### Constructing activities for background knowledge

When preparing a text for the classroom, it is important to identify what background knowledge is absolutely essential in order to understand it. Once you have identified this, you can construct activities to help learners gain this knowledge. The four stages of preparation are:
1   Identify the background knowledge incorporated in the text.
2   Assess whether learners are likely to have this background knowledge.
3   Assess whether the background knowledge is essential for an understanding of the plot or characters.
4   If it is essential, design a task that will help learners access this background knowledge.

**Try this** ☞

### Using paintings and music to build background knowledge

An additional way into the poem by Wilfred Owen would be to work with paintings of the sacrifice of Isaac (e.g. by Titian, Caravaggio, and Rembrandt, all of which make a good contrast). Alternatively, find a recording of Benjamin Britten's *War Requiem* and play your class his setting of the poem. Leonard Cohen's song, *The Story of Isaac*, also refers to the same story. Either play it to your class or study the lyrics as a poem with students. (See Chapter 9 for more suggestions for using art and music to build background knowledge.)

## Integrating background knowledge using factual texts

With poems and short stories, it is often quite easy to integrate background knowledge into the main lesson. With novels and plays, you may need to think of other approaches. If you are studying a novel where you feel that the social and historical background is essential, it may sometimes be necessary to devote whole lessons to building learners' background knowledge and then connecting it to the text they are studying. In most cases, you will be using factual texts which provide the necessary knowledge, and there are different ways of constructing tasks to help learners acquire this knowledge.

### Using a 'test-yourself' technique

Find a number of texts from history books or online sources that discuss the period. Construct a multiple-choice quiz, ensuring that the answers to the questions are in the texts being used. Ask students to test themselves first, and then check the answers in the texts you have provided. For example, here are two questions that were used in a quiz about WWI, in conjunction with *A Farewell to Arms* (1929) by Ernest Hemingway.

1  In WWI, Italy:
   A  fought against Austria and Germany.
   B  was an ally of Austria and Germany.
   C  was neutral.

2  The USA entered WWI in:
   A  December 1916.
   B  April 1917.
   C  November 1917.

In this case, the first question was constructed because it was assumed that many learners would (wrongly) think that B is the correct answer based on their knowledge of WWII, whereas in fact A is the correct answer. For the second question, the answer can very easily be found with an online search.

## Integrating intertextual knowledge

*Animal Farm* (1945) by George Orwell is probably one of the most famous literary texts to be based on actual historical events, and it is interesting to consider the different types of knowledge that may be needed to understand it. Many readers know that the plot of the 'fairy story', as Orwell called it, is based on the history of the Soviet Union in the two decades or so following the Bolshevik revolution in 1917. What is interesting is the extent to which Orwell referenced very specific events in Russian history. Jeremy Myers, in his book *Orwell: Life and Art*, provides a very detailed account of the way Orwell did this. Again, the temptation is for the teacher to provide this information in the form of a lecture, but a more effective way is to make this into a task, providing learners with the historical information and asking them to find the corresponding passages in *Animal Farm*. Below are four examples of historical quotes which learners can be asked to find parallels for in *Animal Farm* (answers given in brackets).

1   From each according to his abilities, to each according to his needs.
    CRITIQUE OF THE GOTHA PROGRAM *BY KARL MARX*

    (*'But everyone worked according to his capacity'*, Chapter 3, p.18.)

2　The Communists openly declare that their ends can be attained only by the forcible overthrow of all existing social conditions. Let the ruling classes tremble at the Communist revolution. The proletarians have nothing to lose but their chains. They have a world to win. Working men of all countries, unite!

THE COMMUNIST MANIFESTO *BY KARL MARX AND FRIEDRICH ENGELS*

(This is paralleled by the sentiments of Old Major's speech in Chapter 1, p. 5, in lines such as *'What then must we do? Why, work night and day, body and soul, for the overthrow of the human race!'*)

3　Hymn To JV Stalin
The world has no person
Dearer, closer,
With him, happiness is happier
And the sun brighter.

ORWELL: LIFE AND ART *BY JEFFREY MEYERS* 2010

(The poem *'Comrade Napoleon',* which compares Napoleon's eye to *'the sun in the sky'*, Chapter 8, p. 63.)

4　I arranged long walks for Alexei Maximovich, I was always arranging bonfires. The smoke of the bonfire naturally affected Gorky's weak lungs.

TESTIMONY AND CONFESSION OF MAXIM GORKY'S SECRETARY AT BUKHARIN'S TRIAL, MARCH 1938.

(In Chapter 7, p. 57, two sheep confess to murdering an old ram *'by chasing him round and round a bonfire when he was suffering from a cough'*.)

Below is a similar activity constructed for *The Brooklyn Follies* (2005) by Paul Auster. It focuses only on extracts from the novel which refer to other works of literature. This is to help learners to understand how much the novel deals with literature and with creative impulses, and to appreciate the richness of the intertextual references that occur in it.

Rather than simply giving information to the students, we construct a simple matching task where students decide which literary quote from *The Brooklyn Follies* (in the left column) matches which explanation (in the right column). Explain that there may be more than one match for each quote.

| | |
|---|---|
| 1) … before long the quartet had decided to band together and form a group. They called themselves Brave New World … (p. 72) | a) A famous French children's book |
| 2) As Oscar Wilde once put it, after twenty-five everyone is the same age … (p. 80) | b) An Irish writer in the first half of the 20th century |
| 3) … I was still curious to know if my other Holmesian theories were valid or not. (p. 91) | c) A 19th-century Anglo-Irish playwright, famous for his wit |
| 4) 'Are you telling me you're married to a man named James Joyce?' (p. 91) | d) Shakespeare's *The Tempest* |
| 5) … like the Little Prince marooned on his rock in the middle of space. (p. 100) | e) A novel by Aldous Huxley |
| 6) What empty dolts we mortals be. (p. 102) | f) A fictional detective who has become mythical |

**Answers:** 1 d, e; 2 c; 3 f; 4 b; 5 a; 6 d

TABLE 3.1　*Intertextual references from* The Brooklyn Follies

**Try this** ☞ **Intertextual references (1)**

If you are working with *The Brooklyn Follies* or another work rich in intertextual references (e.g. Salman Rushdie's *Haroun and the Sea of Stories*, discussed in Chapter 6), do a matching exercise for references in the first quarter or third of the novel, and use other types of tasks for references in the rest of the novel.

**Try this** ☞ **Intertextual references (2)**

Once you have identified a number of intertextual references with students, suggest that they might try and look for others. Assign different sections of the novel to different groups with the mission of detecting how many intertextual references they can find.

## Integrating background knowledge about writers

At some point in your teaching you may decide that you want to provide learners with knowledge about the writers that you have studied or that you are going to study. As mentioned in Chapter 2, this is not necessary for an aesthetic experience of reading, but it can enrich both learners' reading and their experience of working with literature.

**Try this** ☞ **Matching portraits**

Using online sources, find photographic and painted portraits of a number of different writers. Ask students to match the photos to the paintings. This works well if you find portraits from different periods in the writer's life. Writers who have been photographed or had their portrait painted many times include Charles Dickens, Henry James, and Virginia Woolf.

**Try this** ☞ **Describing writers from portraits**

Use a photographic or painted portrait of a writer and ask students to write a short physical description. If necessary, provide various adjectives for the students to choose from. You could also ask students to compare a portrait of a writer with a written physical description from a biography or autobiography. Another variation on this activity is to find written descriptions of different writers and ask students to match them to actual portraits. Include more descriptions than portraits, or vice-versa, to make this slightly more challenging.

✓ *Getting it right*    **Scaffolding activities for learners**

As with other tasks, learners may need some scaffolding and guidance when they look at portraits of writers. If so, suggest they consider the following questions:

1  Do you recognize the writer? If so, what do you know about them? What works have they written?
2  Can you tell from the writer's clothes and setting what century it is?
3  Does the writer look rich/poor; happy/sad; successful/unsuccessful; other?
4  Is the person clearly a writer, or might they have another profession as well?
5  What else would you like to know about the writer?
6  How would you find out more information about the writer?

## Integrating background knowledge using project-based work

When the background knowledge that learners need is well-defined and circumscribed, you can design a project for them to explore the knowledge needed. A good example is *The Curious Incident of the Dog in the Night-Time* (2003) by Mark Haddon, where an understanding of Asperger's Syndrome can help learners appreciate the issues that face the central character and narrator of the novel, Christopher. Instead of bringing to class a list of behaviours associated with the syndrome, you can ask students to research it and present their findings. Either provide them with websites to do this (see page 139), or get them to find websites on their own.

A slightly different way of going about this would be to remind students that Christopher plans to go to university, and to direct them to one of the websites mentioned on page 139. Their task could be to write a short guide for university staff, incorporating their findings.

## Creating cross-curricular units

In some cases, you may be able to create whole units of study that will provide the background knowledge for a text that you are studying. Although an intimate knowledge of Florence and Italy is not necessarily needed for an appreciation of *A Room with a View* (1908) by EM Forster, it can be enhanced by knowing the places and understanding the various geographical, historical, and artistic references to medieval and Renaissance Florence. There are a number of areas of background knowledge that feature in this novel such as a general knowledge of Italy, including:

- Historical knowledge about Florence in the Renaissance (e.g. Guelfs, Ghibellines, Savonarola, Lorenzo de' Medici)
- Italian artists (Giotto, Fra' Angelico, Luca della Robbia, Luca Signorelli)
- Geographical knowledge of Florence (Arno, Lungarno, Santa Croce, Piazza della Signoria)

Although none of these areas are essential to an understanding of the plot or indeed of the characters, many of them are worth knowing in their own right. You could construct a unit of teaching around this, and include some of the following activities:

- Matching exercises such as the ones for *Animal Farm* and *The Brooklyn Follies* on pages 52–53.
- Asking students to research one of these areas, providing them with specific names of artists or historical figures.
- Using a map of Florence and asking students to locate the different places mentioned in the novel as they read it. They should also be able to find photos of most of these places online and may be able to 'reconstruct' some of the scenes in the locations where they take place.

Another area of background knowledge in *A Room with a View* is an understanding of the different customs and behaviours that govern the lives of the characters in the novel. It may be difficult for learners in the 21st century to imagine European pre-WWI conventions, but sensitizing them to this could be done with a short questionnaire such as the one in Table 3.2.

|  | True | False | Not sure |
|---|---|---|---|
| 1 A young woman could travel abroad on her own. | | | |
| 2 A young woman could travel abroad with an older, female chaperone. | | | |
| 3 It was highly offensive for an unmarried man and woman to kiss, whether in public or in private, unless they were engaged. | | | |
| 4 Wearing wild flowers in your hair was acceptable in polite society. | | | |
| 5 Mentioning intimate matters such as having a bath was not acceptable in polite society. | | | |
| 6 Talking to strangers about the effects of food or matters such as indigestion was not acceptable in polite society. | | | |

**Answers:** 1F, 2T, 3T, 4F, 5T, 6T

TABLE 3.2    *Questionnaire on European pre-WWI conventions for* A Room with a View

## Learners' previous literary knowledge

In the various activities and tasks presented in Chapters 1 and 2, there was an assumption that learners would be acquainted with the different genres of literature, at least in their L1. The concept of genre is an important term in literary studies, although you may not necessarily expect learners to use the word. Essentially, genre refers to different categories of writing, with the traditional categories being poetry, prose and drama. Today, we normally identify more genres than this according to length, subject matter and approach. Within prose, for example, we usually differentiate novels, short stories, essays, thrillers and several more. Although all societies and cultures have examples of most genres, different cultures may have preferences for different genres. Below we suggest a number of activities to make learners more aware of the different genres they have encountered – or will encounter.

**Try this** ☞    **Exemplifying genres (1)**

Table 3.3 can be used to elicit students' knowledge of literature and literary forms. You can ask them to do this individually, in pairs, or in groups. Example answers are provided in the right-hand column but you can delete some of these depending on students' likely knowledge. (The example answers are canonical rather than modern, but you can add more recent examples.)

| Literary genre | Example in L1 | Example in English |
|---|---|---|
| Novel | | *David Copperfield* by Charles Dickens<br>*Lord of the Rings* by JRR Tolkien |
| Poem | | *If* by Rudyard Kipling<br>*The Road Not Taken* by Robert Frost |
| Play | | *Hamlet* by William Shakespeare<br>*All My Sons* by Arthur Miller |
| Short story | | *A Christmas Carol* by Charles Dickens<br>*A Garden Party* by Katherine Mansfield |
| Autobiography, memoir | | *The Long Road to Freedom* by Nelson Mandela<br>*Miracles of Life* by JG Ballard |
| Biography | | *Life of Samuel Johnson* by James Boswell<br>*Eminent Victorians* by Lytton Strachey |
| Essay | | *Of Travel* by Francis Bacon<br>*Shooting an Elephant* by George Orwell |
| Letters | | *The letters of Virginia Woolf* |
| Diaries | | *Diary of Samuel Pepys*<br>*The Diary of a Young Girl* by Anne Frank |

TABLE 3.3  *Examples of literary genres*

**Try this** ☞ **Exemplifying genres (2)**
Assign each genre to a different pair or group of students and ask them to research it online, find examples for it in English and in their L1, and report back.

**Try this** ☞ **Most/least favourite genres**
In small groups, ask students to discuss which genre(s) they like most or least of those listed in Table 3.3. They should give reasons for their answers.

**Try this** ☞ **Writers and genres**
In teams, students write down the names of as many novelists, poets, and playwrights that they can think of (in any language and from any historical period). The team with the longest list wins. This activity also serves to remind students that many writers have written works in more than one genre.

## Revising metalanguage

The **metalanguage** you will use is probably best taught piecemeal, as and when needed: so when you use or teach poetry, you will probably teach words such as 'rhyme', 'rhyme scheme', 'stanza', etc. When you teach a short story or a novel you will be teaching words such as 'plot', 'character', 'characterization', 'narrator', 'narrative', etc. The Glossary on page 137 is a good source for terms you might want to teach at various stages.

**Try this** ☞ **Sorting vocabulary**

One way of teaching metalanguage is to present students with a list of words and ask them to sort it according to a criterion that you provide. For example, with the list below, you could ask students to sort it according to the four major literary genres (play, poem, novel, short story):

| | | | |
|---|---|---|---|
| playwright | plot | rhyme | actor |
| poet | stanza | epic | couplet |
| novelist | character | blank verse | limerick |
| sonnet | script | twist | set |

You can do the same with specific words from a text that you are going to teach, provided there is a clear criterion for sorting. You can also present students with a list of words and ask them to decide on a criterion for sorting.

**Why this works** ⇢

---

**Learning through active processing**

This type of activity is useful for a number of reasons. It builds on the knowledge of the learners – some of them may already know some of the words. Rather than 'teaching' the words (in which case, a student who knows the words might be bored), everyone has to do the same activity – which will be easier for some. Clearly, learners will meet these words later on and this will contribute to remembering them, but having to process the words for meaning at the initial stage will make them more memorable.

---

# Part 2    Working with literary genres

# 4    Short stories

You are very likely to be able to use short stories in your teaching: their length means that they are accessible, language issues are less likely to intrude heavily, and also learners are less likely to tire of them. There are many subgenres of the short story, such as ghost stories, humorous stories, and science fiction. Some short stories are very short indeed; others are almost as long as short novels. We will refer to a number of examples and then focus on two stories – one published in 1895 and one from the 1970s.

## What is a short story?

There is a great deal of terminology defining and discussing short stories, but unfortunately terms can vary in meaning when used by different experts. We will use the term narrative as a general term, with short stories and novels being obvious examples.

Key elements in any narrative are 'What?' and 'Who?' it is about. We may also find answers to the questions, 'When?', 'Where?', 'Why?' and 'How?'.
- **What:** This tells us what has happened and, in a sense, why there is a narrative at all. In short stories, there is usually only one main event, whereas in a novel many events may be narrated.
- **Who:** This refers to the central character or characters of the narrative. They are typically human, but certainly not always, especially in folk tales. Sometimes a lot of description may be given of the characters, in other narratives very little detail at all.
- **When:** When did the key event of the narrative occur? For some narratives this is especially important, for example, in real-life or fictional stories about murder and other crimes, or in stories set in the distant past.
- **Where:** This helps to illuminate aspects of the culture of the characters, perhaps helping to explain why they act or react as they do.
- **Why:** What is the reason for what has happened in the narrative, and why do the characters act as they do? This is not always spelt out but must be inferred by the reader/listener. In some cases it may be the main focus of a story.
- **How:** This provides details of the ways in which events in the narrative came about and can be important, for example, with crime stories. In other cases, it has much less focus.

**Try this** ☞ **Identifying key elements in a narrative**

Ask students to read *An Arrest* (1909) by Ambrose Bierce, an American journalist who disappeared in Mexico in 1913. (For the complete text, see the additional resources on www.oup.com/elt/teacher/itc) Table 4.1 gives the answers to the *Wh*-questions. When you do this activity, leave the answers to only a few of the questions in the table and ask students to complete the rest. Afterwards, discuss whether this story is merely a ghost story or whether there are different explanations for it.

| Who | Orrin Brower, a murderer | Burton Duff, the jailer |
|---|---|---|
| What | Murders his brother in law; is jailed; escapes; is brought back to the jail by a ghost | Is murdered by Orrin Brower; in the form of a ghost, pursues Orrin Brower back to jail |
| When | No specified time; the main events take place over one night | |
| Where | In the jailhouse moving to the forest and to the jailhouse | |
| Why | No reasons are given for the original murder; the escape is for freedom | The appearance of the ghost can be interpreted as Orrin Brower's own fears of being caught or even his conscience |
| How | Escapes by killing the jailer | Catches Orrin Brower by appearing to him in spite of being dead |

TABLE 4.1 *Wh- questions in* An Arrest

## Two systems of narrative analysis

There are many systems for analysing narrative, but initially it is useful to focus on just two: **event structure** vs. **discourse structure**, and the **situation/ problem pattern**.

### Event structure

This refers to the events ('What' and 'When' of the story) as though they were an actual sequence of events, organized chronologically. In other words, if the story is a true one then the event structure tells us what happened, following the order in which it happened. Many simple stories and personal anecdotes follow the event structure. Some critics use the term 'plot' for this.

### Discourse structure

This refers to the sequence of events as narrated by the storyteller. These may deviate from real life: for example, the initial events which trigger what happens later may not be mentioned at first, provoking curiosity and interest on the part of the reader. In murder mystery stories, for example, the story often begins with the discovery of a dead body. The police and other characters then try to reconstruct the prior sequence of events which led to the death. In *An Arrest*, the discourse structure and the event structure are identical. In other stories, however, the two structures diverge, as we shall see in some of the examples below.

**Try this** ☞ **Event structure vs. discourse structure (1)**

*Filboid Studge, the Story of a Mouse That Helped* (1911) is a typically quirky and witty story by Saki. (For the complete text, see the additional resources on: www.oup.com/elt/teacher/itc) The first part gives the basic introductory details of the story, but not in event structure. Ask students to reorder the event structure, based on the following discourse structure.

1  Mark Spayley asks Duncan Dullamy if he can marry his daughter.
2  Dullamy is pleased at Spayley's request.
3  All of Dellamy's recent business projects have failed.
4  One product, in particular, a breakfast cereal, Pipenta, has done very badly.
5  Dullamy agrees to the engagement.
6  Spayley asks how he can help Dullamy.
7  Dullamy asks Spayley to market Pipenta.

> Answers: 3, 4, 1, 2, 5, 6, 7

The story continues with Spayley successfully marketing Pipenta and making a fortune for Dullamy, but as with many short stories, there is a twist at the end!

**Try this** ☞ **Event structure vs. discourse structure (2)**

The contrast between event structure and discourse structure can also be demonstrated by using the first two paragraphs of the short story *Eveline* from the collection *Dubliners* by James Joyce (see Text 4.1, with the sentences in the second paragraph numbered for easy reference). One task is to ask students to put the sentences in the order in which they happened. (This would give an order of 3, 5, 6, 7, 8, 9, 4, 10, 11, 1, 2, 13.) Another task is to ask the students to categorize each sentence and decide whether it refers to the present, the recent past or the distant past. (This would give the following pattern: 1–2: present; 3: distant past; 4: recent past; 5–9: distant past; 10–11: recent past; 12: no time period referenced 13: present/future.)

Understanding this discourse structure, through tracking the many sentences that refer to the past, can help students understand the way in which Eveline is trapped. A similar pattern can be found in many other paragraphs in the story.

> She sat at the window watching the evening invade the avenue. Her head was leaned against the window curtains and in her nostrils was the odour of dusty cretonne. She was tired.
>
> [1]Few people passed. [2]The man out of the last house passed on his way home; she heard his footsteps clacking along the concrete pavement and afterwards crunching on the cinder path before the new red houses. [3]One time there used to be a field there in which they used to play every evening with other people's children. [4]Then a man from Belfast bought the field and built houses in it – not like their little brown houses but bright brick houses with shining roofs. [5]The children of the avenue used to play together in that field – the Devines, the Waters, the Dunns, little Keogh the cripple, she and her brothers and sisters. [6]Ernest, however, never played: he was too grown up. [7]Her father used often to hunt them in out of the field with his blackthorn stick; but usually little Keogh used to keep nix and call out when he saw her father coming. [8]Still they

> seemed to have been rather happy then. [9]Her father was not so bad
> then; and besides, her mother was alive. [10]That was a long time ago;
> she and her brothers and sisters were all grown up; her mother was
> dead. [11]Tizzie Dunn was dead, too, and the Waters had gone back to
> England. [12]Everything changes. [13]Now she was going to go away like
> the others, to leave her home.

TEXT 4.1    *Extract from* Eveline *(1914) by James Joyce*

## Situation/Problem pattern

This system of analysis considers the typical elements of narratives.
Some *Wh-* questions can be mapped on to this, with the elements or stages
as follows:

- **Situation:** Who? Where? When?
- **Problem/Complication:** What? or What happens?
- **Solution:** What is done to try to resolve the problem?
- **Result:** What happens next?
- **Evaluation:** How successful is the resolution?

In simple stories, the elements are likely to be in this order, which is
that of event structure. More complex stories may change the order.
We demonstrate how this can be used in our discussion of Kate Chopin's
story, *The Kiss*, later in this chapter.

## Preparing to teach short stories

It is important to choose a story that you personally like and will be able to
work with for several lessons. Clearly, it also needs to be at the right level for
learners in terms of language and interpretation. There are three important
points to consider when choosing a short story to teach.

### 1  Culture

Most stories are embedded in a particular local or national culture.
In Chapter 3, we mentioned *The Luncheon* by WS Maugham, where
to appreciate the tension experienced by the narrator, the reader has
to understand the convention of ordering different courses. Essential
preparation for studying this story would involve getting some sample
menus for Western-style meals. In groups, students could compile some
menus and exchange their experiences of eating in restaurants.

### 2  Chunking

A very useful technique when dealing with short stories is to present them in
chunks or sections. The chunks will often correspond to different paragraphs
in the original, and may sometimes (but not always) correspond to stages or
elements in the situation/problem pattern. If possible, copy each chunk on a
separate piece of paper, giving it out in the relevant lesson. If the text is only
available in the students' books, ask them not to read or look ahead. You can
also ask them to physically cover the text so that their eyes aren't drawn to
later paragraphs.

Why this works ▐▐▐▶

> ### Making the story manageable and meaningful
>
> With chunking, the text is broken up into shorter, manageable sections for teaching and studying. Also, at the end of each chunk you can ask: Is this the end of the story? Answering this involves discussion of the essential ingredients or stages of a story, and of what makes the reader feel satisfied that a story is complete. Learners thus develop their sense of the short story genre, and of narrative more generally. You can also ask predictive questions at the end of each chunk: What will happen next? Do you think x, y or z will happen? You can also ask questions which involve returning to the text as revision and consolidation: What have you learnt about the characters so far? How would you like them to develop? What would you like to happen to the characters?

### 3  Language work

In general, learners should be encouraged to read fairly quickly through each chunk in order to get the gist of what is happening. Later on, tasks will invite them to look back at particular parts of the text. Not all unknown vocabulary and structure can be discussed; some must be left unexplored, so long as the main points of the story have been understood. However, in any story, there are likely to be certain words or phrases which turn out to be significant in the story, help to differentiate characters, and indicate a climactic moment, etc. Learners need help at the appropriate time to find these and understand their significance. When you choose a short story to teach, it's important to clarify to yourself beforehand which words are essential for understanding and which can be discussed only if learners focus on them.

## Example lesson sequence: *The Kiss*

*The Kiss* is a short story published in 1895 in *Vogue* by the American writer, Kate Chopin. (For the complete text, see the additional resources on www.oup.com/elt/teacher/itc) There is little in the story to show that it was written at the end of the 19th century, apart from the language in some cases, and the reference to receptions and teas as the main social events for the characters in the story. Learners might be surprised to discover that it was written so long ago.

There are three characters in the story: a woman and two men. The woman wants to marry one of the men, but seems to be involved with the other. All three characters apparently spend their lives in social pursuits. The writer gives considerable detail about their characters and actions. Through their actions we can perceive their thoughts and emotions. There is also a lot of dialogue, but no description of the physical setting, apart from a very general description of the room in the opening chunk.

The story can be broken up into five chunks onto which we can map the answers to the *Wh-* questions and elements of the situation/problem pattern. In printed versions of the text, there is a clear break between Paragraphs 14 and 15.

| Chunk | Paragraphs | Event and discourse structure | Situation/Problem pattern |
|-------|-----------|-------------------------------|---------------------------|
| 1 | 1–3 | What, Who, When, Where | Situation |
| 2 | 4–10 | What, Who, When, Where, Why | Problem |
| 3 | 11–14 | What, Who, When, Where, Why | Solution |
| 4 | 15–18 | What, Who | Result |
| 5 | 19–20 | What, Who | Evaluation |

TABLE 4.2   *Narrative analysis in* The Kiss

Work through the story a chunk at a time. If you are devoting entire lessons to the story, you will be revealing a number of chunks in each lesson, and students will be reading these chunks in class. Alternatively, you can devote 15–20 minutes each lesson to the story and ask students to read the chunks at home.

## Chunk 1 (Paragraphs 1–3)

Introduce the story very briefly, giving only the title. Hand out the first chunk for students to read at home (or read it together in class), but don't reveal how many chunks there are in total.

When the class next meets, briefly check students' general understanding and enjoyment. Don't worry if all details and vocabulary haven't been understood – much of this will become clearer to the students as they work through the activities suggested below.

Organize students into groups. Ask them to decide which of the *Wh-* questions is answered in the chunk and which stage of the situation/problem pattern it represents. Ask them to suggest what might happen next.

**Why this works** ⏵

> **Active analysis through discussion**
>
> By working through these analytical points, students get at the main points of the story. For example, the 'Who?' is the two characters so far introduced, the 'When?' is late afternoon in winter ('fire in the grate', 'dull light'). 'Where?' is less clear but also less important. By delving into the text and discussing the points, students are both practising language and getting to understand the content and structure of the story. This is more effective than them simply trying to answer a set of comprehension questions. Through the discussion, it may become apparent which key vocabulary items and grammatical structures are problematic. Students can either resolve this collaboratively or the teacher can help.

## Chunk 2 (Paragraphs 4–10)

Ask students to read the chunk at home. At the next class meeting, check whether they have any urgent questions, and decide whether it is appropriate to deal with them immediately or not. Then, in groups, students should again decide which of the *Wh-* questions is answered in the chunk and which stage of the situation/problem pattern this is (see Table 4.2). This should lead to discussion of the possible solution: What will Nathalie do? In addition to 'What?', 'Who?', 'When?', and 'Where?', Chunk 2 also provides a 'Why? to explain Brantain's confusion and Nathalie's anger.

Ask each group to make notes about each of the three characters of the story, writing down what is said about their actions and personality. Alternatively, each group can choose one character to focus on, highlighting in the text what is said about the character, and then summarising this in a table, later to be shared with groups representing the other characters.

Table 4.3 is completed for Chunks 1–3. Decide how much of this information you want to remove for students to complete for themselves. (As indicated, it is not possible to complete the information for every section of the table.)

| Nathalie | Brantain | Harvy |
|---|---|---|
| She sat in firelight. She was handsome and composed, with strong colouring. She occasionally glanced at Brantain. | He sat in shadow, which gave him courage. | — |
| She knew Brantain loved her. | He was frank and didn't conceal his feelings. | — |
| She wanted to marry Brantain; she liked his wealth. | He looked insignificant and unattractive, but was rich. | — |
| — | — | He was young. He entered the room, striding up to Nathalie and kissing her. |
| She got up quickly. | He got up more slowly. | He looked amused, defiant, and confused. |
| She held out her hand to Brantain, but couldn't speak. | He was uncomfortable, and stammered when speaking. | — |
| She spoke angrily to Harvy. | — | He spoke coldly, in self-justification. |
| She spoke frankly and engagingly to Brantain. | He was unhappy but cheered up a little. | Nathalie described Harvy as an old family friend. |
| She seemed close to weeping. | He cheered up more. | — |
| She was triumphant. | He was radiantly happy. | — |

TABLE 4.3    *Notes about the characters in* The Kiss (*Chunks* 1–3)

### Chunk 3 (Paragraphs 11–14)

As before, ask students to read the chunk at home. This time, asking 'What?' is particularly important. Students should continue to add to the table. Ask them to speculate whether this is the end of the story. Nathalie is engaged to marry Brantain, as she had hoped and planned, but what about her feelings and those of Harvy?

### Chunks 4 and 5 (Paragraphs 15–18 and 19–20)

These two chunks are shorter than Chunks 2 and 3; either read them in class or assign them to be read at home, working in a similar fashion to the previous chunk. Paragraph 18, the last paragraph of Chunk 4, suggests that Nathalie intends to continue her involvement with Harvy. Stopping here and asking students whether this is the end of the story forces them to read this paragraph carefully and understand Nathalie's plan better. Asking them what will happen next will elicit interesting responses.

Chunk 5 is particularly interesting: Paragraph 19 includes Harvy's evaluation of what has happened; Paragraph 20 includes Nathalie's evaluation of what has happened and of her future.

To help students understand these two evaluations (and before you present the chunks), ask half the class to write a paragraph about what Harvy thinks about what has happened, and the other half to write a paragraph about what Nathalie thinks. You can mention that the technical term for this is **evaluation** and that it refers to the result of the previous actions.

Form pairs of students: one has written about Harvy, the other about Natalie. Ask students to read their paragraphs to each other and see how they would fit as an ending to the story. Discuss the various endings with the class and then reveal the original ending. Ask students to compare their endings with the original and discuss any differences or similarities.

As a final activity, you could have a class discussion and evaluation of the story, and address any language points that have arisen during the lessons. You could also connect *The Kiss* to some of the activities presented around the theme of love and marriage in Chapter 2.

**Why this works** ▐▌▌▌➡

> ### Creative writing as critical analysis
>
> This type of activity forces learners to go back through the story, reread it, and make judgments about where it would lead and about the characters' points of view. For example, Nathalie's evaluation of the result is predictable, as she has achieved what she set out to do. She also seems aware of what she has had to give up for a wealthy husband, and – despite a degree of disappointment for her – the price is worth paying. Harvy's evaluation is less predictable, and not totally transparent: What does he mean when he says that kissing women is dangerous? Does he mean the physical act of kissing a woman? Or does he make a judgment of women and their behaviour in general? This activity thus requires quite close reading of the text, but without learners realizing that this is what they are doing.

**Try this** ☞ **Looking at different reactions**

Use the following reactions to the story (elicited from our friends and family) to elicit students' thoughts and responses. (Note that, interestingly, one of the readers thought this was an extract from a longer work; this validates the points that we made earlier about chunking and the procedures for using it.)

### Readers' reactions

1  The Kate Chopin excerpt seems to me, despite its rich language, cheap, a 'dime novel'. I feel I read it (or some equivalent) when I was a teenager, and if it wasn't me it was a teenage (likely female) friend who did and told me about it.

2  I did like it. I don't know how old it is but think that it was about her greed for comfort and how it robbed her of loving someone as she clearly didn't love her husband. A tale of what happens frequently, especially in this day and age.

3  Enjoyed the read but took a real dislike to both characters. I thought he was weak and questioned why he loved her (just for how she looked?).

And I found her cunning and shallow. The writing was atmospheric and vivid. I could picture the scenes and rooms very clearly.

4  I didn't find it particularly engaging, perhaps as it is only an extract, but it didn't pique my interest in any of the characters or their predicaments. I found the descriptions a little trite, and the writing style disjointed.

5  There is something no-nonsense about this. It's a story that could happen now, it's a story as old as time. I like the way it is being told.

6  The piece made me feel uncomfortable. I felt sympathy and pity for Brantain, who was being manipulated without knowing it. He is not as emotionally intelligent or emotionally adept as Nathalie. To me, Brantain is vulnerable and sensitive while Nathalie is manipulative, cunning, and measured.

**Try this** ☞ **Interviewing a fictional character**
Ask students, in groups, to check the character notes in Table 4.3. Each group should then focus on one particular character, imagining that the character is going to be interviewed by a journalist about their actions and intentions. Form pairs from different groups. In each pair, one student role-plays the journalist, and the other student role-plays the character. The pair then switches roles.

**Try this** ☞ **Dramatizing the story**
Using the dialogue given in the text, ask students to dramatize the story, adding any necessary words and also perhaps shortening and modernising the language. Students can act their versions in front of the class, or record them to play back or share online.

**Try this** ☞ **Silent film scene**
While a lot of dialogue is given in the text, there is also considerable description of the physical actions of the characters. Ask students to imagine a silent film of the story or a scene from it, and then prepare and act a dramatization. In this story in particular, the basic relationships between the characters and the meanings of their actions come over even without dialogue.

**Try this** ☞ **Chat show**
Ask students to focus on one character, their motivation, and their view of what has happened. Students should then imagine that the three characters are being brought together by a chat show host who is intent on pitting them against each other. Ask four students (one for each character, and one for the chat show host) to act out the encounter.

**Try this** ☞ **Updating the story**
Ask students to rewrite the story for the 21st century. What would happen? How would the motivation of the different characters be different?

**Try this** ☞ **Writing a sequel/continuation of the story**
This is particularly appropriate for this story, as Nathalie is clearly someone with a very different view of marriage than her husband. Asking students to write a sequel requires them to show their understanding of her scheming character.

## Example lesson sequence: *How Soon Can I Leave?*

*How Soon Can I Leave?* (1973) by Susan Hill, also the author of the horror novella *The Woman in Black*, is a longer short story which would take up a number of lessons. It concerns two unmarried women who live in a British seaside town, and is a marvellous text for many kinds of pedagogical exploitation. Like *The Kiss*, it can be broken up into chunks. (For the complete text, see the additional resources on www.oup.com/elt/teacher/itc)

### Chunk 1

Introduce the story very briefly, without revealing its length and whether the first chunk is in fact the whole story or not. Ask students to read the chunk at home to get a general idea of the content. Remind them that it's not necessary to understand every word (e.g. 'raffia', 'trestle').

When the class next meets, start by establishing clearly the 'Who?', 'Where?', 'When?' of the story (the situation), beginning with the details of the main characters. They are clearly differentiated, and the differences between them and their experiences turn out to be important in the story. It is essential for students to get a clear grasp of each character, and so we suggest devoting two exercises to it.

Real-life texts in which personal details are requested or shown include such documents as job advertisements, missing person notices, obituaries, and passport or other travel documents. We can take one of these as a model, using it to trigger the extraction of relevant information from the text.

We learn later in the story that the two characters, Miss Roscommon and Miss Bartlett, plan a trip to Italy and so what is suggested here is completing a table which asks for passport-type information for both women. Not all the questions would be asked these days, for example, 'Skin colour' and 'Special features' (e.g. a scar or other facial marks), so we are using pedagogic licence here and extending the categories to include character.

Ask students to try to complete as much of the passport information for Miss Roscommon and Miss Bartlett as they can. This can be done individually or in pairs, followed by group discussion.

| Passport information | Miss Roscommon | Miss Bartlett |
|---|---|---|
| Family name | | |
| First name | | |
| Marital status | | |
| Age | | |
| Place of residence | | |
| Occupation | | |
| Height and physique | | |
| Skin colour | | |
| Special features or aspects of character | | |

TABLE 4.4   *Passport information for Miss Roscommon and Miss Bartlett*

**Points to note**

- Miss Roscommon doesn't appear to have a first name. Why is this? What would culturally appropriate names be? Suggestions from learners in the past include Martha, Dorothy, and Matilda.
- Miss Bartlett's name, Mary, is given in Chunk 2. This can be added to the table later.
- Two ages are given for Miss Bartlett in the story: she is forty when she comes to live with Miss Roscommon, and then forty-seven when the story as such begins (where the 'Problem' is presented).
- The two women live in Miss Roscommon's house in the seaside town of Mountsea. The house is called 'Tuscany': it is an old tradition for houses in Britain to have names. These can indicate details of the place (e.g. Seaview, Tall Trees, etc.) or remind the owners of a favourite holiday location (e.g. Tuscany, Tenerife, etc.).

 **Getting it right**

**Inferring from the text**

Before doing this activity, discuss with students where they can find the answers. Some of the answers can be found directly in the text, which requires students to scan the whole text and carefully read particular parts of it. However, some of the answers can't be found directly in the text, so explain to students that they need to infer, or even to invent information. Encourage students to discuss any disagreements openly and to support their choices.

**Why this works** ▐▐▐▶

**Developing literary sensitivity**

From one point of view, this is a straightforward and traditional comprehension exercise which has been made more purposeful as each answer helps to build up a new text, namely the passport information. But this exercise also serves to heighten learners' sensitivity to literary works. Filling in the gaps which the author has left is an important part of reading and reading comprehension. It represents the early stages in the development of literary competence. Discussing choices and defending them heightens learners' awareness of these choices and their appropriacy.

Having established many of the basic facts about the two characters, we can delve a little into their personalities – into how they might regard themselves and how they might be regarded by others, including the reader.

In pairs, ask students to assign the adjectives below to one or both of the women. A few adjectives may apply to neither woman. Students don't need to agree on their allocation of the adjectives: these are not objective descriptions but evaluative ones, and what is important here is the process of choice and the discussion. If appropriate, students can also suggest two or three additional suitable adjectives.

| | | | |
|---|---|---|---|
| helpless | lonely | rich | practical |
| decisive | artistic | bossy | snobbish |
| happy | secretive | good at cooking | mature |

Discussion of possible answers reveals that the two women are probably not very self-aware. Some explanation might be needed for some words, for example, 'artistic', and at this point students might need to be told (or shown, using a photo) what 'raffia' is.

To conclude work on this chunk, we suggest asking students, either individually or in groups, to consider an evaluation question and a predictive question.

### Questions

1   Who is the story about? Both women equally, or one of them? If only one, which one? (This might provoke some discussion, but more of the paragraphs are devoted to Miss Bartlett.)

2   Is this the end of the story? If not, how do you think it will develop? What will happen next? (Some students may suggest that this chunk could be a complete story, which gives a description of the two characters with some hint at tensions, which are unresolved or accepted. Other students will see this extract as the first part of something longer.)

## Chunk 2

The first sentence of this chunk suggests a turning point, a complication, or a problem. More characters are introduced and more dialogue. There is a lot going on here, suggesting opportunities for discussion of aspects of culture, for language practice, for general discussion, and for dramatization.

### Focus on culture

There is a great deal in this story which depends on knowing and understanding cultural behaviours. For example, we pointed out earlier that in Britain, some people name their homes, which may be unfamiliar to learners in other countries. Another example of the cultural elements in this story is the attitude to food, feeding other people, and the social conventions related to meals or refreshments generally. You will have to make decisions about introducing or explaining different customs which appear in the story, partly according to the distance from learners' own culture.

---

**Try this** ☞ **Family meal**

Ask students to imagine that some relatives they haven't seen for many years are visiting their house for a family meal. In groups, they could discuss one or more of the following questions:

• What will you give the relatives to eat and drink?
• How do you think everyone will behave?
• What will everyone talk about (and avoid talking about)?
• Try to decide some of the things that they will actually say.

Points which might come up include the following:

• Key food items for a family reunion meal in students' home cultures.
• Norms of formal and informal behaviour in a family group, including whether everyone waits for the most senior person/male to speak first, whether it is customary to eat first and then talk or vice versa.
• Culturally safe topics at such a gathering, for example, the guests' journey, favoured relatives who are not present, recent weddings, and funerals.
• Topics to avoid, such as politics, religion, personal finances.

**Try this** ☞   **Formal tea**

Ask students to research typical food items for a British 'formal tea' (sandwiches, scones, butter, cream and jam, fruit cake, small cakes, iced buns, tea with milk or lemon, etc.). Ask them to choose their favourite food from the descriptions they can find. Which food would/wouldn't they like to try? Are they surprised by any of these foods? Do they have similar foods or occasions in their own culture?

**Why this works** ⫸

> ### Cultural topics as language practice
>
> It is often helpful to examine your own culture and make cultural assumptions explicit. The activities above encourage learners to move away from considering their own culture as the norm or 'the best'. Additionally, all of this provides learners with good language practice in the form of reading (e.g. when researching typical items for a formal tea) and in the form of discussion, through presenting and defending their points of view.

*Focus on language*

The activities we suggest above all involve language work to some extent. The story also provides numerous opportunities for more focused and explicit language work. These can be done as individual, pair-work, or group tasks.

**Try this** ☞   **Working on reporting vocabulary**

Ask students to substitute all the instances of 'said' in the text with one of the following reporting verbs:

| | | |
|---|---|---|
| protested | announced | exclaimed |
| explained | commented | insisted |
| stated | declared | informed |

You can also ask students to suggest additional suitable words.

**Try this** ☞   **Identifying meaningful repetition**

As you study any story, you may spot meaningful repetition that adds to the understanding of the characters or the situation. An example in this case is that the writer refers to each of the four characters as 'flushed'. Ask students to check the dictionary meanings of 'flushed', find the references in the text, and suggest what it indicates in each case. What does each use reveal about the characters? Another meaningful repetition in this text is the reference to both Angela and Miss Bartlett (twice) as 'cat-like'. Similarly, ask students to find the references and discuss what they mean. Are they complimentary?

**Try this** ☞   **Reviewing previous views of characters**

Ask students to review what they previously thought about the characters. Would they change or add to any of the adjectives which they allocated to the two women in the activity on adjectives in Chunk 1?

**Try this** ☞   **Practising polite phrases**

Use the dialogue in the story to create an extension activity using polite phrases. For example, you could practise some of the phrases used during eating and drinking (Could I offer you some more … ?, Would you like some more … ?, Could you pass me the … ?, etc.), and some conversational clichés (I don't know if you've heard …, Did you ever hear/meet/see … ?, etc.).

**Why this works** ▐▐▐▶ | **Consolidating learning**

As well as practising learners' vocabulary, these activities force them to go back into the text and think more about how the characters are feeling and what they are saying. Asking learners to change or add to previous work they have done helps them understand the development of characters as events unfold. This helps them consolidate their learning (both linguistic and literary) in a natural way.

### *Focus on drama*

Chunk 2 lends itself particularly well to a number of drama activities. There are different ways in which you can get learners to dramatize some of what occurs in this section, and different ways in which you can support them in doing so.

**Try this** ☞ **Public vs. private selves**

It is clear that the characters don't all say what they think, apart perhaps from Miss Roscommon, who is always very direct. Tell students that they should split the characters into two: their polite public selves and their private selves with their inner thoughts. Working in groups, students should form pairs, each pair sharing one of the characters. One member of each pair should prepare to act the character as he or she appears to the others, using the dialogue as given in the text, plus any additions. The other member should act the inner thoughts of the character.

**Try this** ☞ **Awkward family meal**

Ask students in small groups to devise and then act out a short scene at an awkward family meal. As guidance, ask them to decide what the meal is (e.g. a weekday dinner at home, a special celebration, or entertaining distant relatives). Ask them to clarify the relationships between the characters and to think about the language each character is likely to use.

**Why this works** ▐▐▐▶ | **The importance of repetition**

Drama techniques in general are good fluency activities. Importantly, because they also involve performance in front of others, learners first practise and rehearse what they are going to dramatize. This means that the rehearsal and repetition essential to language learning are done in a naturalistic way.

The first activity above serves to summarize and revise understanding of the story. It also forces students to read between the lines, and to verbalize what is being left unsaid in the story: the **subtext**. The second activity takes students beyond the story, into their own lives, potentially using words from the story. By acting a similar situation in their own context, they are better able to understand the tensions that arise in the story.

## Chunk 3

A good way to start this chunk is with a predictive question (which also serves as a revision of the meaning of the previous chunk): Do you think Miss Bartlett will leave? This chunk presents a solution to the problem of Miss Bartlett feeling that she needs to leave Miss Roscommon's house. The result is that Miss Bartlett experiences yet more problems. These new problems are triggered or caused by the weather.

Ask students in pairs or groups to complete one or more of the following tasks:

1  Complete Table 4.5. Decide how much of this information you want to remove for students to complete for themselves. (As indicated, it is not possible to provide information for every section of the table.)

| Types of weather (and date, if given) | Miss Roscommon's reaction | Miss Bartlett's reaction |
| --- | --- | --- |
| The wind blows round the walls of Miss Bartlett's house. | — | Relief. She is alone in her own home at last. She no longer hears Miss Roscommon's breathing at night. |
| Miss Roscommon comments that Miss Bartlett's house is not warm. | Sends blankets and a Dutch apple pie. | — |
| 7th November: storms | Sends a meat pasty and a note to Miss Bartlett. | Throws the pasty away and tears up the note but thinks of the comforts of 'Tuscany', Miss Roscommon's house. |
| 9th November: gales | Visits the cottages and hammers at the door. Leaves flask of lentil soup. | Hides upstairs. |
| More storms | — | Lies in bed, terrified. Decides to return to 'Tuscany'. |

TABLE 4.5    *Types of weather and reactions in Chunk 3*

2  Find and highlight or underline all references in the story (both in this chunk and in previous ones) to Miss Bartlett's mother. How has she affected Miss Bartlett?

3  Discuss what Miss Bartlett has learnt through the events of the story.

4  Discuss whether this is the end of the story.

## Chunk 4

This final chunk is very short – and sad. Ask students to read it in class silently and to wait until everyone has finished reading before giving any reaction (or ask them to note their reactions in writing immediately after finishing their reading). After dealing with any queries, get students in their groups to discuss their reactions and evaluation of the story. Ask again what Miss Bartlett has learnt, as well as what they think is the overall meaning of the story.

## Rounding up the story

There are some examples of rounding-up work on literature in Chapter 2. Here we provide two activities specifically connected to food to use with *How Soon Can I Leave?*

The many food references in the story particularly relate to Miss Roscommon, who prides herself on being a good cook and, more broadly, on being a good house-keeper, manager, and carer. Being competent in these ways seems to justify her existence. She feeds Miss Bartlett well when they both live together, and sends food parcels to Miss Bartlett when she leaves to live in her own house. In this way, Miss Roscommon shows her love for Miss Bartlett. At the same time, Miss Roscommon is rude and insensitive, patronising and upsetting Miss Bartlett by referring to her as *my little pussycat* in front of visitors.

The food that is referred to is traditional British food of the 1970s (when the story was written) and 1950s (when it is set): sandwiches, slab cake (large whole cakes), scones, home-made jam, home-made soup. When on her own Miss Bartlett manages with slabs of cheese and boiled eggs. This simple food makes her feel artistic and above such a humdrum activity as cooking interesting and varied food.

**Try this** ☞ **Function of food in your culture**

Discuss with students the function of food in their culture: Is it different from the function it had a generation ago? Which meals are important in their culture? What does the attitude to food in families indicate about family roles and family dynamics?

**Try this** ☞ **Who eats what?**

Ask students to go back and list all the times that food is mentioned in the story, and see which character each item of food relates to, who prepares it and who eats it. What does this tell them about the different characters?

## Considering the overall meaning

This is an important question to discuss at the end of any story that you read with learners. For most readers, *How Soon Can I Leave?* is a study of the denial of loneliness and neediness. Each woman needs the other, but will not admit it. Miss Bartlett, especially, refuses to face up to the realities of life. She is under the delusion that, even at the age of forty-seven, she can start a new and successful life as an artist. She is still under the influence of her doting mother and treats Miss Roscommon as a mother-substitute. At the end of the story, and too late, their roles are reversed, with Miss Bartlett cradling the dead Miss Roscommon in her arms. The reader must wonder if and how she will cope without her friend.

Of course, the social circumstances in Britain have changed considerably since the time in which the story is set. Today, forty-seven would not necessarily seem too old to start a new career. In this respect, the story needs to be discussed in its historical context, but the main theme of lack of self-awareness is still powerful.

# 5    Poetry

Poetry may well be the earliest form of literature, whether recited or sung. Although we generally encounter it first in print nowadays, features of sound and rhythm are still important and need to be attended to in some way.

A great deal of poetry has been written in English over the centuries and around the world, and it has always been an important genre in the language. However, many language users find poetry difficult: poems often use metaphorical language that takes time to decipher, and even modern poets may sometimes use unusual or old-fashioned language. We discussed a number of poems in Chapters 1 and 2. In this chapter, we continue our exploration of poetry and aim to show that working with it can be fun, and that poems need not be difficult or tricky.

The tremendous variety of poetry in English is a wonderful resource. There are poems of every length, from extremely short ones – which are ideal to begin with – to extremely long ones, which present a challenge. As well as dense and complex poems, whether long or short, there are also many simple ones. Modern poems may sometimes appear to fit this category, especially when they are in colloquial, not 'poetic' language, but they may still be very compressed and allusive. Poems for children and translations of foreign-language poems are worth considering as more easily accessible alternatives. Finally, we might consider texts which are not exactly poems, but are close to them and more accessible. Examples of these are songs, folk songs, and some adverts.

## Focus on language (1)

One aspect of poetic language is verbal creativity. Poets play games with language to delight the reader and to delight themselves. Their games can be treated as puzzles for the reader to decode. These games can be liberating, especially for the non-native learner, for they show that effective poems can contain incomplete sentences, 'faulty' grammar, and misused words – yet still make good sense and give pleasure. Here is an example from an American writer best known as a novelist.

> **Superman**
>
> I drive my car to supermarket,
> The way I take is superhigh,
> A superlot is where I park it,
> And Super Suds are what I buy.
>
> Supersalesmen sell me tonic—
> Super-Tone-O, for Relief.
> The planes I ride are supersonic,
> In trains, I like the Super Chief.
>
> Supercilious men and women
> Call me superficial—*me*
> Who so superbly learnt to swim in
> Supercolossality.
>
> Superphosphate-fed foods feed me;
> Superservice keeps me new.
> Who would dare to supersede me,
> Super-super-superwho?

TEXT 5.1   Superman *(1955) by John Updike*

What is Updike doing in this poem? He is possibly criticizing the commercialization of modern life, where everything has to be bigger and better: super-sized. Or perhaps he is proud of living in a society of supermen? Or maybe he is just enjoying playing with the flexibility of the English language, in particular the prefix 'super-'.

Some of the words he uses include: 'supermarket', 'superhigh', 'Super Suds', 'superbly'. We can see immediately that there are several different kinds of 'super-'. Most often, English uses it as a prefix: it can be added to virtually any noun, adjective, and adverb, suggesting something that is bigger and perhaps better than usual. Some of these compounds are well established, for example, 'supermarket'. Others are invented, but can be understood in context, for example 'superhigh'. In other cases, though, 'super-' is not a prefix. For example, with 'superbly', we can't take away 'super-' and still have a meaningful word, as we can with 'supermarket'. Finally, Updike uses some proper nouns such as the made-up brand-name 'Super Suds', and the name of a real train, the 'Super Chief'. Below is a sequence of activities for this poem – you may decide to do all of them in different lessons, or only choose one or two.

## Teaching *Superman*

1  By way of introduction, do a brief vocabulary-building session in which students suggest all the words they can think of containing 'super-'. Once they have done this, ask them to allocate the words to one of the following two categories:

  a) 'super-' as a prefix, as in 'supermarket', 'superman', etc.

  b) 'super-' as part of an indivisible word, as in 'supervise', 'superstition', etc.

2  Give out copies of the poem, and read it aloud to students. This will help them to hear how the writer is using 'super-' in many combinations and to react to the effect of this repetition, even if the actual meanings of some of the words may still be unknown.

3  Ask students to comment on the types of 'super-' words being used. Can they spot which words are invented and which are in the dictionary? You could choose to complete Table 5.1 with the class, and explain those words that students still find difficult to understand.

| Established words with 'super-' as a prefix | Established words where 'super-' is not a prefix | Writer's inventions | Proper nouns | Invented proper nouns |
|---|---|---|---|---|
| supermarket<br>supersonic<br>superphosphate | supercilious<br>superficial<br>superbly<br>supersede | superhigh<br>superlot<br>supersalesmen<br>supercolossality<br>superservice | Superman<br>Superchief | Super Suds<br>Super-Tone-O |

TABLE 5.1    *Categorisation of 'super-' in* Superman

4  Once students understand the meanings of the words, they can discuss what this poem means to them. Is Updike commenting on modern society or just playing with language? Is he using language play to comment on modern society? You could also discuss the idea that repeating a word many times can make it meaningless – all you hear is the sound.

**Try this** ☞   **Choral reading**

This poem lends itself well to choral reading: it has a wonderful rhythm, and an alliterative tongue-twister in the first line of verse four. (See page 44 for a discussion of choral reading.)

There are many other instances of poetic verbal creativity and language play. Another American poet, e e cummings, is often cited in this context. Four British writers, George Herbert in the 16th century, Lewis Carroll in the 19th century, and Edwin Morgan and Brian Patten in the 20th century, produced poems laid out in the shape of their subject matter (e.g. an altar, a tail, a map of Scotland, and a flock of birds, respectively). On a much lighter level, the humorous verse form of the limerick is often used to play with English spelling and punctuation.

## Focus on poetic literacy

In addition to language knowledge, and skill in reading and listening in particular, another kind of literacy is needed when we approach the study of poems: **poetic literacy**. Even when they are using supposedly 'everyday' language, poets will still normally arrange it in some deliberate pattern of lines and verses; they will certainly use rhythm and may also use rhyme. They are likely to play with grammar and vocabulary in patterned ways. Readers of poetry need to become attuned to all of this. Learners may know much of this from their first language, so you can have an interesting discussion comparing the common poetic techniques of their L1 and English. The task for the poem below, which is presented with gaps, illustrates ways in which learners can be sensitized to the word choices made by poets.

---

**Symphony in Yellow**

An omnibus across the bridge
Crawls like a _____ butterfly,                      pretty / yellow / tired
And, here and there, a passer-by
Shows like a _____ restless midge.                  little / large / tiresome

Big barges full of _____ hay                        ripened / yellow / bundled
Are moored against the _____ wharf,                 busy / bustling / shadowy
And, like a yellow _____ scarf,                     cotton / silken / spotted
The _____ fog hangs along the quay.                 thick / thin / yellow

The yellow leaves begin to _____                    turn / fall / fade
And flutter from the Temple _____,                  elms / oaks / trees
And at my feet the pale _____ Thames                green / yellow / blue
Lies like a _____ of rippled jade.                  path / line / rod

**Answers:** yellow, little, yellow, shadowy, silken, thick, fade, elms, green, rod

---

TEXT 5.2     *Gap-fill version of* Symphony in Yellow *(1889) by Oscar Wilde*

There are several things to note about this activity. Even with the gaps (and ignoring the proposed gap-fillers), the reader can get quite a good idea of what the poem is about. It is a descriptive piece, set alongside the river Thames in London, probably in autumn ('fog', 'yellow leaves'). The title is interesting: How can a poem be a 'symphony', and why 'yellow'? It will help to be aware that Wilde formed part of the Aesthetic Movement at the end of the 19th century, in which poets, painters, and musicians emphasized the links between their art forms. James McNeill Whistler produced paintings which he called, for example, *Nocturne* and *Symphony in White*. Yellow was also an iconic colour at this time, as can be seen in the title of the subversive arts magazine *The Yellow Book*, containing art, prose, and poetry. As a result, we might expect the word 'yellow' to occur several times in the poem.

## Teaching *Symphony in Yellow*

1 Show some of Whistler's paintings to the class, and discuss the images and titles of the paintings. Paintings of London by Claude Monet can also be used here. This could be a good occasion to elicit or teach words such as 'wharf', 'quay', and 'Thames'.

2 Tell students they are going to read a poem that describes a scene with a similar atmosphere to the paintings they have just looked at.

3 Distribute the poem and ask students, individually or in pairs, to fill in the gaps.

4 After a few minutes, stop students (even if they have not finished) and ask how they are managing to do the task. What is influencing their choices? Is it the meaning of some of the phrases or of the whole poem, or is it rhyme and/or rhythm? Hopefully the following aspects of poetic literacy will be elicited:

- Titles are very important and can help the reader interpret the poem.
- A lot of the meaning of a poem such as this can be grasped, even with an incomplete text. In considering the choices for each gap, the reader is helping to 'co-create' the poem, and so will gain a deeper insight into it (and into poetic creation more generally).
- Many poems have clear rhyme schemes. In the first verse, there is 'bridge', 'fly', 'by', and 'midge'. We can represent the rhyme scheme as *a-b-b-a*, which is the pattern for the rest of the poem.
- A less common pattern is that of eye-rhyme, where words look on the page as though they rhyme, but don't when you pronounce them. Wilde uses it in the second verse. The two 'a' lines don't rhyme in sound: 'hay' (/heɪ/) then 'quay', which is pronounced /kiː/; similarly, neither do the 'b' lines: 'wharf' (/wɔːf /) and scarf (/skɑːf /).
- Another tool for the poet is alliteration. Wilde uses it with 'big barges' and with 'lies like'. So, do students think he will follow these with 'bundled' and 'line' – or would that be too much? With the last line of the poem, there's the possibility of a second alliterative pattern: 'rod of rippled jade'.
- **Assonance** is yet another tool, in which vowel sounds rhyme but not consonants. Thus, three lines from the end, 'Temple' (/tɛmpl/) has the same vowel as 'elms' (/ɛlmz/).
- Overall meaning, normal collocations, and real-world knowledge must be considered, even when we know that poets can play with language and imagery. Are midges normally 'large' or small ('little')? Scarves can be 'spotted', of course, but is that image relevant here? The textures implied by 'cotton' or 'silken' are perhaps more appropriate. Is fog normally 'thick' or 'thin'? What colour is 'jade'?
- Rhythm is often important. Midges can indeed be 'tiresome', but perhaps this word, with its triphthong (three vowel sounds) in the first syllable, /taɪəsəm/, is too long for the context.
- Poems can contain iconic words and phrases, which the poet might even over-use, e.g. 'yellow' in this case. In other words, poets are not necessarily always right. At the end of the activity, we might even conclude that some of our word choices are better than Wilde's! This kind of gap-filling can also be done using the poet's own rejected choices, taken from various drafts of the poem (where available). In some cases, readers might think that some earlier options are better than what was eventually published.

 *Getting it right*

**Focusing on the main purpose**

At this stage of the lesson, don't expect to make all of these points! Try and elicit many of them from students, but the main purpose of the discussion at this stage is to highlight to students — and especially those who may be having problems doing the task — what is doable and how to go about it.

5 Now ask students to return to the task. Make the point that they may want to revise their original choices in the light of the whole-class discussion.

6 Put students in small groups to compare their choices and come up with one agreed version of the poem.

7 Three or more groups can be asked to read their final versions. There will always be some differences.

8 Finally, read aloud Wilde's own version and ask students for their reactions and comments. One common reaction is that he has used the word 'yellow' too often!

**Why this works** ⫸

> ### Multimodality and motivation
>
> Paintings and photos are excellent ways into poems (or any text), and can activate motivation and elicit responses which you can then use as a lead-in to the text you are studying. They create cross-curricular connections and highlight these connections to learners. They introduce an important **multimodal** element into the language classroom, and make an important change from language-based, pre-reading activities. Try building up your own collection of images that you find work in class (see also Chapter 9).

## Focus on language (2)

Some poems exhibit a dominant grammatical structure, and so can be useful as a means of revising and utilizing the structure in an interesting context. Obviously, you must allow time to discuss and enjoy the poem for its own sake and there may well be one or two difficult words or structures which will need to be dealt with first.

Poems for children can be entertaining and appropriate in this context, and not too linguistically demanding. Examples are John Keats' *There was a naughty boy*, with its focus on the comparative 'as … as', and Eleanor Farjeon's *Cats*, with its repeated 'any' and 'anybody's' and use of prepositional phrases.

The short seven-verse poem in Text 5.3, *Horse*, is by George Mackay Brown, who lived in the Orkney Islands in northern Scotland almost all his life. The islands are small, low-lying and extensively farmed, with an almost constant view of the sea. The poem presents the essential roles of a horse through the day and through the rural maritime year. Each verse has the same structure. There are no rhymes, and apart from the last verse, where there is a non-finite verb ('quenching'), there are no verbs. The dominant structure is the noun phrase, typically formed of the definite article and the noun 'horse', followed by a prepositional phrase, for example, 'The horse in the field'.

**Horse**

The horse at the shore
Casks of red apples, skull, a barrel of rum

The horse in the field
Plough, ploughman, gulls, a furrow, a cornstalk

The horse in the peat-bog
Twelve baskets of dark fire

The horse at the pier
Letters, bread, paraffin, one passenger, papers

The horse at the Show
Ribbons, raffia, high bright hooves

The horse in the meadow
A stallion, a russet gale, between two hills

The horse at the burn
Quenching a long flame in the throat

TEXT 5.3    Horse *(1981) by George Mackay Brown*

## Teaching *Horse*

1 Show students some images of Orkney (easily available online),
  ploughing by means of horses, a mail boat, and a horse show. Explain that
  these depict the world of the poet and the poem. Ask students to comment
  on the pictures, trying to elicit some of the words that appear in the poem.
  Elicit from students what they know about traditional roles of horses.

2 Explain some of the less well-known words in the poem (e.g. 'casks',
  'furrow', 'peat', 'raffia', 'burn'). Alternatively, do a dictionary exercise with
  students working in groups: each takes one verse and tries to work out the
  location and role of the horse in it, using the dictionary.

3 Each group reports back to the whole class, with the verses being dealt
  with in sequence.

4 At this point, ask students an open question: What do they think the poem
  is about? Is it one horse or many? What links each verse? The repeated
  structure forms a link; the focus on image rather than action perhaps
  suggests a photographic quality: the poem is a series of stills of horses.
  Is the poem a metaphor for anything? Some readers have noticed a thread
  of 'redness' and light through it: red apples and warming rum, perhaps the
  glint of light on the metal plough, fire, paraffin, bright hooves, a red wind
  ('russet gale' in the poem), a flame, etc. Other readers have suggested a
  link with whisky, or with sexuality.

**Try this** ☞ **Creative writing**

Text 5.3 can provide a good model for students to write animal poems of
their own. Besides the horse, a number of other animals have, or have had,
important social and economic roles in different societies (e.g. dogs, cows,
elephants, camels, monkeys, etc.). Individual students could attempt whole
poems, or contribute a verse each, alone or as a small group, to a class poem.
You may also want to show different pictures of animals to stimulate students'
imaginations.

**Try this** ☞ **Deciding how to deal with difficult language**

Because poems are often so short, difficult language can be more of a challenge
for learners than in other genres. You may decide to deal with it at the beginning
by pre-teaching any essential vocabulary, or you could also use it for dictionary
work. Sometimes you can construct an activity with the difficult language that
will lead students to the themes of the text. Alternatively, deal with each word
as it comes up, if and when students need it.

*A Song before Marriage* is a traditional poem from India. It is in simple
language, with a clear linguistic pattern of questions and answers. It lends
itself particularly well to a 'jumbled verses' activity (see Chapter 2).

---

**A Song before Marriage**

How shall I buy
A red and yellow cloth?

How shall I buy, mother
A beautiful girl?

With money I shall buy
The red and yellow cloth

With words I shall buy
The beautiful girl

Where shall I put
The red and yellow cloth?

Where shall I put
The lovely girl?

In a chest I shall put
The red and yellow cloth

In a room I shall put
The beautiful girl.

---

TEXT 5.4  *From D. Thompson* (1978) Distant Voices, poetry of the preliterate

## Teaching *A Song before Marriage*

1  Get students into groups and give each group one of the verses. Ask them to speculate on what sort of poem their verse might be from. What is the poem about? What might come before or after their verse?

2  Ask the whole class for their initial ideas. Establish that some groups have questions and some have answers.

3  Get the groups who have questions to find appropriate answers from some of the other groups.

4  Make new groups containing one representative from each of the original groups. Ask them to try to assemble the whole poem.

5  Tell representatives from the new groups to read out their complete poem. Don't worry if there are different sequences: these can be discussed.

6  If appropriate, discuss the issue of 'buying' a marriage partner.

7  Invite groups to write poems in the same format.

## Focus on sound

Limericks are humorous verses, with a very strong rhythm, which means that they are good for choral chanting and for working on sound. The first two limericks (Texts 5.5 and 5.6) are by the writer who is often credited with inventing the form, Edward Lear. The third is anonymous.

---

**5.5**

There was an Old Man with a beard
Who said, 'It is just as I feared! –
Two Owls and a Hen,
Four Larks and a Wren,
Have all built their nests in my beard!'

**5.6**

There was a young lady whose chin
Resembled the point of a pin;
So she had it made sharp,
And purchased a harp,
And played several tunes with her chin.

**5.7**

You'd require an extremely long scarf
If you happened to be a giraffe.
They get very hoarse
In the winter, of course –
And a sore throat is no cause to laugh.

---

TEXTS 5.5–5.7     *Three limericks (5.5 and 5.6 by Edward Lear; 5.7 by Anon)*

## Teaching limericks

The following sequence can be used for Texts 5.5–5.7.

1 Get students into groups to research images of owls, hens, larks, and wrens, and information about them: What sort of birds are they? What sort of beard do they think the old man has, if he has so many birds' nests in it?

2 Practise saying Limerick 5.5 aloud, emphasizing the rhythm.

3 Get students into groups to read Limerick 5.6, checking any words if necessary. Ask them to read it aloud chorally.

4 Draw students' attention to Lear's typical style: the subject is frequently an old man or young woman; the first and last lines conclude with the same word. (In fact, in many of Lear's limericks the first and the last lines are nearly identical.)

5 Limerick 5.7 breaks away from Lear's formulaic style – as do most modern limericks. Get students to read it silently and then check the pronunciation of 'scarf', 'giraffe', and 'laugh'. While there are different pronunciations for 'giraffe' and 'laugh', which ones must be used to maintain the rhyme established in the first line? Now check the pronunciation of 'hoarse', 'course', (and 'cause'). Finally, ask students to read the limerick aloud in groups.

✓ *Getting it right*

### Sound in poetry

Sound is a very important aspect of any poem. For any poem that you teach, make sure that there is at least one activity which involves the sound. Even if you ask the students to read the poem for the first time silently, make sure that you read it aloud to them at some point, or use one of the activities below.

**Try this** ☞ **Comparing different readings of a poem**

Play a recording of a poet reading their own poem, or an actor reading the same poem. Some poets (e.g. Robert Frost) have produced particularly compelling recordings of their work. For one of the most famous poems of the 20th century, Frost's *Stopping by Woods on a Snowy Evening*, there are many readings. (Please see Useful websites on page 139.) Compare the reading of the poet with that of an actor, or two different actors. You can also ask students to find websites with different readings of the poem you are studying. Ask them to characterize each reading, and teach them the words to do this. Then ask them to choose the two best readings and explain why they liked them.

**Try this** ☞ **Folk songs**

Many, if not all, folk songs and traditional ballads can be seen as poems. There are often different versions of the same songs performed by a variety of singers (e.g. *Mary Hamilton*, also known as *The Four Marys*, or *The Three Ravens*). Ask students about the effects of the different versions.

## Focus on story

Many poems tell a story. In *What has happened to Lulu?* by Charles Causley a story is told about a young woman who has apparently run away from home.

**What has happened to Lulu?**

What has happened to Lulu, mother?
What has happened to Lu?
There's nothing in her bed but an old rag-doll
And by its side a shoe.

Why is her window wide, mother,
The curtain flapping free,
And only a circle on the dusty shelf
Where her money-box used to be?

Why do you turn your head, mother,
And why do the tear-drops fall?
And why do you crumple that note on the fire
And say it is nothing at all?

I woke to voices late last night,
I heard an engine roar.
Why do you tell me the things I heard
Were a dream and nothing more?

I heard somebody cry, mother,
In anger or in pain,
But now I ask you why, mother,
You say it was a gust of rain?

Why do you wander about as though
You don't know what to do?
What has happened to Lulu, mother?
What has happened to Lu?

TEXT 5.8    What has happened to Lulu? *(1951) by Charles Causley*

## Teaching *What has happened to Lulu?*

1 Have an initial class discussion on different reasons why some young people leave home. How would students manage if they were in that situation?

2 Read the poem aloud to students and then give out copies for them to read themselves.

3 Ask who they think is speaking in the poem. Is the narrator a sibling – if so, are they younger or older?

4 Ask students, either in small groups or as a whole class, to compare the poem with the points they made in their initial discussion.

**Try this** ☞ **Lulu's note**

Ask students to write the farewell note that Lulu left.

**Try this** ☞ **Role-play**

Get students to role-play a meeting between Lulu, her parents, and the police or social services.

**Try this** ☞ **News article**

Get students into groups and ask them to write a news article about what happened to Lulu.

**Try this** ☞ **Comparison**

Compare Text 5.8 with the Beatles' song, *She's Leaving Home*. If you decide to teach James Joyce's short story, *Eveline*, (see Chapter 4), you could also refer to it here as a comparison.

**Why this works** ⫸

> **Literature and personal issues**
>
> Leaving home – whether as a realistic prospect or as a fantasy – is an important topic for many young people, and discussing different reactions to the theme has an important educational value. The different points of view – that of the narrator in *What has happened to Lulu?* and the multiple voices of the parents and the girl in *She's leaving home* – provide ample ground for discussion. Comparing different works on the same theme demonstrates to learners that much of literature deals with similar issues, and that these themes are relevant to their own lives and aspirations.

# 6  Novels and longer works

Using a long work such as a novel or a play in the language classroom has many advantages. It allows elements of extensive reading to come into the classroom. It also allows sustained work on one topic, thereby creating a sense of continuity; learners may have read a variety of novels in their L1, and the genre should be familiar to them.

However, using longer works raises specific issues for the teacher. Choosing the work to be studied or used is even more important than when studying short stories or poems, because choosing a work that students aren't keen on will affect a large number of lessons. It is also much more difficult to monitor whether students are reading the text being studied or not. Teachers often feel that they need to provide a larger variety of activities than they do with shorter texts.

In this chapter, there is a particularly strong focus on ways of choosing and setting up the study of a long text, including working with learners to choose the text that they wish to read. We then show how the teacher can check that learners have actually read the text, and demonstrate how it is possible to come up with a variety of activities. We refer to a number of contemporary works as well as to earlier 19th century and 20th century ones.

## Choosing which texts to use

A number of factors are likely to influence the choice of a longer work to study with your class. We look at those which many teachers have indicated are important, with some suggestions about how they can be dealt with when making your own selection.

### Length

Most teachers consider the length of a novel as the first and most important consideration. Even when the language is not very difficult, they feel that learners would be intimidated by a book that looks long to them. This means that for many teachers, works by key authors such as Dickens or the Brontës are in effect excluded – some teachers would never choose them whilst others will study parts of the novel in detail, but skip other parts.

If you only have time to use one long text, choose one that is 150–200 pages long. This should not be too intimidating. There are also texts that are even shorter, for example, *The Body* by Hanif Kureishi (approx. 120 pages), or *Of Mice and Men* by John Steinbeck (approx. 100 pages). Many modern novels written for young adults are quite short – if you are teaching more than one text, start with the shortest one and then move on to longer and more complex texts.

## Topic

The topic is crucial in terms of appealing to learners. In many contexts, but most likely in school settings, teachers want to introduce important social topics to learners through the texts that they choose – for example, migrants and asylum seekers and their treatment by society, which is the main theme of *The Other Side of Truth* (2000) by Beverley Naidoo. *The Body* (2003) by Hanif Kureishi is a futuristic story of the ultimate transplant calculated to achieve immortality – transplanting the brain. With elements of a science-fiction story, it raises important issues about our attitudes to our bodies, to life and to death. *Pig Heart Boy* (1997) by Malorie Blackman deals with issues of transplantation, animal rights, and teenage friendships. Broadening learners' horizons, and introducing them to countries and cultures that they may not know are all factors influencing the choice of text.

**Try this** ☞ **Cross-curricular connections**

Choose a text that is connected with some of the other areas that the school curriculum focuses on. You will be able to work on cross-curricular themes and also show learners how literature reflects many areas of life and illuminates them. Some possibilities are *Animal Farm* (1945) by George Orwell to connect with the Russian revolution; *To Kill a Mockingbird* (1960) by Harper Lee to connect with issues of racism and civil rights; *Empire of the Sun* (1984) by JG Ballard to connect with WWII.

## Appeal to the learner

The age, gender, and general attributes of learners are important factors. In secondary schools, teachers have for many years chosen novels whose protagonists are young people (e.g. *The Catcher in the Rye* by JD Salinger). Increasingly, teachers are choosing **young adult (YA) literature**, a genre which focuses on works specifically written for teenagers, such as *The Curious Incident of the Dog in the Night-Time* by Mark Haddon and *Noughts and Crosses* by Malorie Blackman.

If you are not sure what will appeal to your class, choose a text that has universal appeal – a contemporary YA novel will probably work best for most classes. Alternatively, find ways of involving your students in the choice (see below).

## Appeal to the teacher

This is not always mentioned in lists of factors influencing choice, but is just as important as the others. If you choose a novel to teach, you must really like it as you will be reading and rereading it, and spending a great deal of time on it. If you are not enthusiastic about your choice, then your lack of enthusiasm will transfer to learners. Our advice is simple: make sure that you choose a work that you really like!

## Availability of a good student edition

Some teachers like to work with student editions which have a glossary, notes, and guiding questions for learners. Great care, however, needs to be exercised here: some student editions are quite heavily annotated and at first glance look very different from a normal novel or text of a play. The implicit message that learners might get is that novels are there only to be exploited and studied in detail, rather than to be enjoyed and engaged with, and only later explored.

If possible, choose 'light-touch' student editions, with not too much annotation or explication. Language work and interpretation can be handled in class, using available resources or those that teachers themselves put together.

### Availability of support material for teachers to work with

Working with a novel will take up a large number of classroom sessions, and it is therefore important to provide variety in the type of activity used in class. This will probably mean that teachers have to construct many of the activities on their own. In such cases, it is always a good idea to choose a novel that has already generated some critical attention. Novels from the literary canon will have anthologies of critical essays devoted to them, which makes it easier for teachers to create activities and also provides teachers with some sort of a standard of critical understanding that they can aim at getting learners to achieve. For more recent novels it is helpful to find book reviews, many of which are available online.

### Achieving variety

In contexts where learners need to study a number of works, teachers often want to ensure that there is a variety of genres. Genres you can use include autobiographical novels (e.g. *The Absolutely True Diary of a Part-time Indian* by Sherman Alexei), science-fiction (e.g. *Frankenstein* by Mary Shelley), and magical realism (e.g. *Life of Pi* by Yann Martel). You can also choose novels where different narrative techniques are used, such as letters in *The Guernsey Literary and Potato Peel Pie Society* by Mary Ann Shaffer and Annie Barrows, and the choice of a dog as a narrator in *Timbuktu* by Paul Auster.

### Availability of a film

This can be an important factor, especially in situations where learners are not particularly motivated to read longer texts. The film can then be used in a variety of ways to help learners engage with the work and understand plot, characters, and themes.

If you have any doubts whether learners will enjoy the study of literature, make sure that for at least one of the texts you use, and possibly the first one, there is a corresponding film. (See Chapter 8 for how to combine the study of literature and film.)

## Involving learners in the choice

Some teachers choose the text for study themselves, but many involve learners in this process. Of course, the more advanced learners are, the easier it is to involve them in the choice, but it is also possible to involve intermediate learners as well. There are many different ways to do this, and one of them will probably work for you.

**Try this** ☞ **Providing a menu of choices**

Bring the books you are considering for study to class, together with blurbs, summaries of the plots, and any other information that might help students choose. They can then spend one or two sessions discussing the different possibilities and agreeing a choice. This can give rise to many speaking and reading activities, and can also widen students' knowledge of literature through superficial acquaintance with novels and plays.

**Try this** ☞ **Students providing possible choices**

Ask students to bring in books that they have heard of or that they are interested in reading. This works well in small classes, but it can also work in larger classes because often not every student will bring a book for consideration. You can also ask them to find reviews and summaries of the book (either from print or online sources) and bring those along as well. Another possibility is to ask students to suggest or bring in books that they have read in translation in their L1, and which they think might interest their peers.

**Try this** ☞ **Relying on past students' views**

Ask students from previous years to come and talk to the students; alternatively, collect opinions from students and use them in subsequent years to help students choose a text. Each book you consider could be accompanied by notes and recommendations from past students.

**Try this** ☞ **Students taking full responsibility**

If you are working with an advanced class and your students are highly autonomous, try giving responsibility for choosing a book to students themselves. In some cases, they could read all the books from a pre-selected set (either one which the teacher has constructed, or one prescribed by the curriculum), and then decide together which book they wish to study in depth.

**Why this works** ▥▶

> **Promoting student autonomy**
>
> Very often, classrooms are places where learners perform actions which have been determined for them by others. Involving learners in choosing the texts you are studying is important because it makes them responsible for their own learning, thus increasing student autonomy. It also increases student motivation, as their investment in their learning grows. The process also teaches the skills involved in negotiating and reaching a joint conclusion.

## Introducing the work

Once the text has been chosen, you will be faced with decisions about the first few lessons. If the class has chosen the book, then in many cases they will have read the book already or have some knowledge of its content and you can go directly into dealing with themes and analyses of characters and plot. On the other hand, if the class has not read the book, then the nature of the first lesson should be dictated by the book itself, and some initial activities that work well with one text may not work so well with another. Here are some generic activities that you can use with different books; for each activity we suggest a number of appropriate books.

## Prediction activities

### Predicting from book covers

The first thing we see of a book is its cover – even the title is probably noticed after we have a general impression of the cover. In the classroom, covers can become an important way of generating knowledge about the book to be read. Many novels, even contemporary ones, appear in different editions and with more than one cover. Consider using the different covers as part of a prediction activity (which activity will depend on the actual book you are using). Even if the cover of the edition that learners have is not particularly interesting, and provides little in the way of visual stimulus for classroom activities, the internet makes it easy to access a variety of covers for the same book. You could also include covers of translated versions in different languages. The similarities between covers can help learners identify important themes, topics, or characters in the book; the differences add more information that can be used for prediction. Some covers will be literal; others will be abstract or oblique. Both types are suitable for prediction activities, though the type of prediction may be different (e.g. an abstract illustration on the cover may help in predicting mood; a literal cover will help in predicting plot).

FIGURE 6.1    *Covers of* The Curious Incident of the Dog in the Night-Time

---

**Try this** ☞    **Two covers; one novel**

For *The Curious Incident of the Dog in the Night-Time* by Mark Haddon, show the two different covers in Figure 6.1. Ask students what they actually see on each cover, and how the objects and people on the covers might be connected. Elicit a few predictions about the book from the title and the covers.

**✓ *Getting it right***

**Finding different book covers**

Finding different covers to use in class is relatively easy. Doing an online search for the title of the novel and the word 'covers' will normally direct you to a number of useful websites. If the novel is a well-known one, it will have had many covers over the years, and there may be specific websites comparing the covers. Even a more recent novel such as *The Brooklyn Follies* (2005) by Paul Auster has at least four different covers – but you may need to look for them on different websites.

### *Creative writing as prediction*

As an alternative to brainstorming prediction, you can use creative writing tasks to serve as a more extended introduction. In this case, learners are asked to write down in detail what they think will happen. They can predict using the covers, and you can also supply quotes from the book – either full sentences or phrases – to help learners predict and to introduce new vocabulary.

**Try this ☞**

**Creative prediction**

Tell students to use their dictionaries to find out which words in the list below are connected to storytelling and what they mean. Then ask them to use the cover of *Haroun and the Sea of Stories* (1990) by Salman Rushdie and at least three of these expressions from the book to write a short story. (You may wish to discuss with students some of the elements of a short story, as presented in Chapter 4.)

brand-new saga                    sugar-and-spice tales
a legend comes to town            narrative activities
up-beat sagas                     cancelled his subscription
gloompuss yarns

**Why this works ‖‖➡**

**Creating interest in a text**

Pre-reading activities are particularly important when you are using a longer literary text. Predicting the content of a book through brainstorming can serve as a quick introduction which generates interest in further reading. Predicting activities can also be used to teach unusual, difficult, or thematically important vocabulary. Creative writing activities generate involvement and investment in the lesson and also provide a purpose for reading – learners are always interested in comparing what they wrote to the work they are going to read.

 **Getting it right**

## The first chapter

The next step after a prediction activity is to spend some time reading the first chapter of the book. The first chapter of *The Curious Incident of the Dog in the Night-Time* appears below, followed by some discussion questions. In many classes, learners are able to tell very early on that the narrator provides inappropriate detail and that he may well be autistic. When this comes up, it is best not to react or confirm the learners' suggestions, but rather probe to see why they think this is the case. What is interesting is that very few learners comment on the fact that the first chapter of the book is Chapter 2! The best way to proceed is probably to read the next chapter, Chapter 3, and discuss which questions are answered, and whether any new questions are raised for learners. (By this point, most learners understand that the narrator is a teenager, and that he may have some behavioural difficulties.)

---

### 2

It was 7 minutes after midnight. The dog was lying on the grass in the middle of the lawn in front of Mrs Shears' house. Its eyes were closed. It looked as it if was running on its side, the way dogs run when they think they are chasing a cat in a dream. But the dog was not running or asleep. The dog was dead. There was a garden fork sticking out of the dog. The points of the fork must have gone all the way through the dog and into the ground because the fork had not fallen over. I decided that the dog was probably killed with the fork because I could not see any other wounds in the dog and I do not think you would stick a garden fork into a dog after it had died for some other reason, like cancer for example, or a road accident. But I could not be certain about this.

I went through Mrs Shears' gate, closing it behind me. I walked onto her lawn and knelt beside the dog. I put my hand on the muzzle of the dog. It was still warm.

The dog was called Wellington. It belonged to Mrs Shears who was our friend. She lived on the opposite side of the road, two houses to the left.

---

> Wellington was a poodle. Not one of the small poodles that have hairstyles, but a big poodle. It had curly black fur, but when you got close you could see that the skin underneath the fur was a very pale yellow, like chicken.
>
> I stroked Wellington and wondered who had killed him, and why.

TEXT 6.1    *Extract from* The Curious Incident of the Dog in the Night-Time *(2003) by Mark Haddon*

### Questions

1   Who is the narrator? Are they male/female? How old are they? Why do you think that?
2   Look at the detail that the narrator provides. What does that tell you about the kind of person they are?
3   What questions do you have as a result of reading this chapter?

### *Discussing themes*

Sometimes the theme of the book can be discussed before reading as a way of generating interest. Such discussions not only introduce the main themes of the story, but also provide an opportunity to introduce some background knowledge and vocabulary. The following questions can be asked as an introduction to Rushdie's *Haroun and the Sea of Stories*:

### Questions

1   Why do people like hearing stories?
2   Why do people like reading stories?
3   Do you know someone who tells stories well?
4   Who were the great storytellers of the past?

Learners don't necessarily need to be told in advance that a particular theme you are exploring links to the novel they are going to read – this point can come later on.

### *Starting with the text*

In some cases, there may be even less preparation needed, and learners can be thrown into the text 'at the deep end'. *Of Mice and Men* by John Steinbeck starts with a short description of a clearing in a forest. It is important in the story, because the peace and quiet of this setting are in stark contrast to the events of the novel, and because that is where the story will end – tragically. This beginning lends itself extremely well to a visualisation activity, asking students to learn to see in their mind's eye what they are reading – indeed, the 'natural' way to start this novel is probably for learners to simply close their eyes and to listen to you reading the first few paragraphs of the story, visualize the scene, and then draw it.

Another novel where immediate engagement with the text itself is possible is *The Other Side of Truth* by Beverley Naidoo. The novel begins with Sade, a twelve-year-old girl in Lagos, packing her school bag. She hears shots and a speeding car: her mother has just been murdered. This is a powerful opening which can be used to elicit reactions from learners both to the contents and to the stylistic device which Naidoo uses to differentiate memory from storyline.

 *Getting it right*

**In at the deep end or not?**

When learners have chosen the book according to the cover(s) or reviews, then they will have some knowledge of the plot, characters, and theme. In such cases, you may not need elaborate pre-reading activities. In other cases, if the class knows nothing about the book, then spend some time reading and rereading the first chapter or two. Consider whether you could introduce the class to the novel 'at the deep end' by reading the first few pages, or whether it is worth constructing a pre-reading activity to highlight themes, predict content, or teach vocabulary. Remember that different books will lend themselves to different types of activity.

## Managing the reading

In most cases, it is impossible to read the whole text in class. This means that the teacher needs to decide how to divide up the text for reading. One of the main questions is whether learners should read the whole work before studying it, or read it piecemeal as they study it at the same time. Oddly enough, the latter method is one where there is often less of a 'dip' in motivation or enjoyment in the course, because the teacher is not constantly revisiting ground that learners have already covered. It is also often a function of how well learners are supposed to know the text. In school-leaving exams, they are often required to know the text extremely well and to be able to recall details from it, so teachers feel that they need to cover every detail in the novel.

In other cases, teachers feel that learners can cope without reading every chapter in detail, or sometimes even without reading some chapters at all. In such cases, different parts of the novel can be dealt with differently. Some chapters will be read at home, but key chapters will be read in class; for example, with *Haroun and the Sea of Stories*, learners could read Chapters 1–3 at home, but it is advisable to read Chapter 4 in class because it is crucial for achieving an understanding of everything else that happens in the book.

If you are spending a long time on a novel, and you feel that reading each chapter in detail could present a challenge to your learners, you can assign each chapter to a different group to read in sequence. Each group then teaches their chapter to the rest of the class. This means that the whole class understands the plot and are supported in reading their chapter, but students do not have to read in great detail each week, and different groups have a more detailed knowledge of specific chapters.

**Why this works** ▭▶

> **Utilizing the structure of a novel**
>
> The decision to read Chapter 4 of *Haroun and the Sea of Stories* in class, mentioned above, shows how the structure of the novel was taken into consideration when managing the reading. A different example is *Of Mice and Men*, which is divided neatly into six fairly short chapters, resulting in what are quite manageable chunks for learners (though some teachers further divide each chapter into two sections). Using the structure of the novel to manage the reading allows time to think about specific sections and understand the place of each section in the novel. It also uses the signposts that the author intended for readers to note.

✓ *Getting it right*

> **Using structure to manage the reading**
>
> When you read the novel in preparation for teaching, think about the way in which its structure will help in managing the reading. Take into account the following questions:
>
> 1 How can the division into chapters help?
> 2 Do the chapters fall into clear groups or sections?
> 3 Are there different strands to the plot that can help divide the reading between groups of learners?
> 4 Are there chapters that are less important for the development of the plot and that can therefore be simply summarized by you or by different groups of learners?
> 5 Are there any chapters or sections that are essential to a clear understanding and therefore must be dealt with in class?

## Providing a variety of activities

When you are using a long text, achieving a variety of activities is important. In this section we discuss a number of standard activities which can be applied and adapted to work with almost any novel.

### *Summary activity*

This activity is designed to help the teacher check whether learners have read the assigned chapter(s) and to assess how well they have understood what they have read; it also works well as a revision activity.

Ask students to discuss in small groups what they have read. Then ask the groups to write a short summary of one chapter for others to read. (This can be done with a laptop or tablet and projector, or with an interactive whiteboard.) Tell students to incorporate one factual mistake in their summary.

After students have written their summaries, project them and read them aloud to the rest of the class (or ask one of the group members to do so); the other groups have to find the mistake in each summary. What is remarkable about this activity is how much learners enjoy it – it appeals strongly to their competitive and game-loving side.

### Acting scenes from a novel

This activity can be done in class or as homework, and there are various options. You can decide for students which part of the text should be dramatized or leave the decision to the students themselves. The dramatization can use dialogue from the book or students can be asked to dramatize sections where there is less dialogue, and where they are required to fill the gaps left by the author.

### Writing definitions of people or objects

Ask students to choose people or objects from the book and define them; then they can present the definitions and see if the rest of the class can guess what they refer to. Again, you can either decide for students what they will define, or leave the decision to them. For example, when working on *Haroun and the Sea of Stories*, students can be asked to define characters (e.g. Butt the Hoopoe, Prince Bolo, Goopy, and Bagha) or objects (e.g. the Disconnecting Tool, the Ocean of the Sea of Stories).

### Choosing favourite quotes

Ask students to choose their favourite quote from a specific chapter (or a group of chapters, or even the whole book). In groups, students then discuss their chosen quotes and decide on one quote that the group thinks is the best or their favourite. You can also ask each student to choose two or three quotes – this then leads to more extended discussion. This is a variation of a classic pyramid activity which moves from individual work to group work and then sharing with the class.

### Walkabout activity with quotes

Choose a number of quotes from the chapter(s) you are currently discussing, print them, and stick them to the walls. Students then walk around the classroom and stand next to their favourite quote. In groups, they discuss why they chose this particular quote and then summarize their decisions for the whole class. This can also be done at the end of the reading as a review of the novel as a whole.

### Writing a blog post or diary entry

Asking learners to write a blog post or diary entry for one of the characters works well with almost any novel. It can even work with novels that are in themselves a diary (e.g. *The Curious Incident of the Dog in the Night-Time*), where learners can write a blog post for one of the other characters.

### Producing visual representations of important scenes

While most activities tap into the intellectual and linguistic abilities of learners, this activity works with learners' personal and emotional reactions, as well as visual and creative elements of responding to a novel. For homework, ask students to draw an important scene or find photos online for characters and locations. You may also ask for a comment on the photos – this can either be submitted in writing to the teacher or presented orally to the class.

### Asking learners to create their own activity

Learners at all levels and of all ages are often extremely creative at coming up with interesting ideas for activities of their own. One group we taught constructed a board game based on *Haroun and the Sea of Stories*.

In another class, one learner recorded a comment on Lewis Carroll's *Alice Through the Looking-Glass* and read this comment backwards, as in a mirror image. Learners often want to create short films or trailers based on their reading; it also possible for learners to create websites, or even video games and virtual worlds based on the work they have read.

### Reading aloud

We discuss reading aloud in detail in Chapter 2. The point to make about it when studying a novel is the importance of choice. There may be specific passages in the book which you might consider reading aloud. These include passages which are essential to ensure that learners understand what actually happens; particularly well-known parts of the text, to increase familiarity; or passages with more than one voice, where there are different accents involved.

# 7  Drama

Drama is found in every society, going right back to ancient times. Greek drama of the 5th century BC, for example, is still performed and highly regarded today. Drama can be silent, as in mime, but we will obviously focus on plays with words.

The English language has a rich dramatic tradition, involving playwrights from all parts of the English-speaking world. This chapter is arranged chronologically, starting with some of the work of William Shakespeare, even though he wasn't the first English language dramatist. We then look at an extract from a work by a late 17th-century female dramatist, Aphra Behn, before moving to the late 19th century and on to the 20th and 21st centuries. The plays are mostly comedies, but the last two are a social commentary and a fairy-tale with psychological undertones, respectively.

Given the nature of drama, it is important that you and your learners should go beyond the printed text and experience it as a play, either through acting some of it, by going to the theatre to see a production, or through watching a film version. If you involve learners in acting a play, much of it can be done as group work, with students taking on a variety of roles: actors, directors, script advisors, designers, etc. Follow-up activities can extend into what is not explicitly shown in the play (the subtext), or into presentation in a different form, for example, the writing of reviews and blog posts.

The extracts we have chosen share several themes. One is that of the outsider or outcast: a person alienated from society because of poverty and perceived social class, or because of religion, race, or skin colour. Several of the plays we consider have a theme of thwarted love, or love which doesn't run smoothly – until the very end, that is!

## Focus on early 17th-century drama: William Shakespeare

Shakespeare is not easy to deal with. Many native speakers of English find his language difficult, even alien. Many words and many cultural practices of his time need to be explained. There are, however, many editions of Shakespeare's plays, including editions designed for use in UK schools. We would recommend using these: not only do they contain clear explanations, but also many good suggestions for individual and class activities. It is also essential for learners to see a film, DVD, or online recording of any play that they are studying.

A whole play by Shakespeare will take a long time to work through in class (see Chapter 6 for general suggestions about using longer works). Because of the language difficulties involved in teaching Shakespeare, consider providing an overview of the play at the outset, with information and class activities, and then dealing with the play in instalments (chunking). Alternatively, you could consider watching a film of the play first, and then moving to work with the text.

## Teaching *Twelfth Night*

*Twelfth Night* is a comedy by Shakespeare. The title refers to the celebrations for Epiphany on 6th January – the twelfth day after Christmas and the traditional end of the festive period. The play was probably written in 1600 or 1601 and has a number of themes. Twelfth Night celebrations have a carnival aspect, in which the world seems to be turned upside down. Misrule is the order of the day: lord or lady becomes servant, and servant becomes lord or lady. People take on disguises and nothing is as it seems. This was common knowledge to the audience in Shakespeare's time, and is reflected in the play. A second theme, found in all of Shakespeare's comedies, is that of love at first sight. A third theme is that of identical twins and the confusion they cause. This is found in other Shakespeare plays: for example, *The Comedy of Errors* depends on two sets of identical male twins. In *Twelfth Night* there is a pair of boy-girl twins, who are obviously not identical, but for the purposes of the play we have to assume that they can be confused. Finally and specifically in this play, there is the theme of the treatment of mad people.

**Try this** ☞ **King or queen for a day**

As preparation for work on the play, ask students (as individuals or in groups) to discuss and then act what they would do if they were king or queen for the day, with full powers to command anything they decide. How would they change their world? There may also be local customs to which you can connect this theme: for example, some schools let students be teachers and administrators for a day. Ask your students to come up with a set of rules for a 'king or queen for a day' event.

**Try this** ☞ **Discussing views of love**

Ask students, in pairs, to discuss the statements in the list below. Do they have any personal experiences to support what they say? Do they think things were different in the past? Are there any statements that are not acceptable in the 21st century? (If you have an advanced class, you could discuss feminist criticism and how it would view such statements.) Many of these statements would apply to any and all of Shakespeare's comedies, but Statement 5 is specifically raised in the play.

1   It is possible to fall in love at first sight.
2   You should get to know your partner well before marriage.
3   People should seek marriage partners from within their own social class.
4   People who are in love are temporarily mad.
5   A man's love is stronger than a woman's: it lasts longer and endures greater adversities.

**Try this** ☞ **Talking about twins**

Ask students to consider how twins are regarded in their society. Do they know – or know of – any identical twins? Have they caused any confusions? Has anyone got an amusing anecdote to tell the group?

**Try this** ☞ **Sayings and proverbs**

Ask students, in groups, to discuss the traditional sayings and proverbs in the list below. Are they a reliable guide to behaviour? (While all of these are relevant to *Twelfth Night*, many also apply to other Shakespeare plays, for example, *A Midsummer Night's Dream*.) One way of structuring the discussion would be to ask each group to choose the saying that they agree with most, and the saying they agree with least. Another way of conducting the discussion would be to use a walkabout (see Chapter 2).

1  Seeing is believing.
2  Actions speak louder than words.
3  Beauty is in the eye of the beholder.
4  First impressions count.
5  Appearances are deceptive.
6  Be what you would seem to be.

Having established the general themes of the play, it is then appropriate to focus on each act in turn, with review sessions from time to time. Here we consider a short extract in which Viola, who is disguised as a young man, is sent by her patron, Count Orsino, to woo Lady Olivia on his behalf. Viola begins with her prepared speech, but Olivia is unimpressed. In fact, she is bored with Orsino and uninterested in his attentions. Olivia's disdain angers Viola, who is in love with Orsino herself. Viola challenges Olivia's attitude and describes movingly how she would behave towards the person she loves. Viola's ardour and energy electrify Olivia and, in an instant, Olivia falls in love with him/her!

**Try this** ☞ **Go-between**

Ask your students to imagine that a female/male friend has asked them to act as a 'go-between' and tell a boy/girl that they are interested in a relationship. How would they do that?

Now watch the following scene on a DVD, or read it aloud to the class before giving out the extract for students to read.

> **Olivia**  How does he love me?
> **Viola**  With adorations, fertile tears,
>       With groans that thunder love, with sighs of fire.
> **Olivia**  Your lord does know my mind; I cannot love him:
>       [1]Yet I suppose him virtuous, know him noble,
>       Of great estate, of fresh and stainless youth;
>       In voices well divulged, free, learn'd and valiant;
>       And [2]in dimension and the shape of nature
>       A gracious person: but yet I cannot love him;
>       He might have took his answer long ago.

> **Viola**   ³If I did love you in my master's flame,
> With such a suffering, such a deadly life,
> In your denial I would find no sense;
> I would not understand it.
> **Olivia**   Why, what would you?
> **Viola**   ⁴Make me a willow cabin at your gate,
> And call upon my soul within the house;
> Write loyal cantons of contemned love
> And sing them loud even in the dead of night;
> Halloo your name to the reverberate hills
> And make the babbling gossip of the air
> Cry out 'Olivia!' ⁵O, You should not rest
> Between the elements of air and earth,
> But you should pity me.
> **Olivia**   You might do much.
> What is your parentage?
> **Viola**   ⁶Above my fortunes, yet my state is well:
> I am a gentleman.
> **Olivia**   ⁷Get you to your lord;
> I cannot love him: let him send no more;
> Unless, perchance, you come to me again,
> To tell me how he takes it. Fare you well:
> ⁸I thank you for your pains: spend this for me.

TEXT 7.1   *Extract from* Twelfth Night *(1602) by William Shakespeare*

Ask students to match Phrases 1–8 in the extract to a–h in modern British English.

a) I come from a good family, but we've fallen on hard times recently.

b) If I loved you as he does, I would ignore your protests.

c) I believe he's a good and noble man; wealthy, young and chaste, with a good reputation.

d) Here's a tip – thanks for your trouble.

e) You wouldn't be able to ignore me or have any peace.

f) Go back, tell your boss to forget it; unless of course you yourself came back to tell me how he takes it.

g) I would hang about near your house, sing love songs and shout out your name and force you to take notice of me.

h) He's a graceful, even handsome man, but I can't love him.

**Answers:** 1c, 2h, 3b, 4g, 5e, 6a, 7f, 8d

---

**Try this** ☞   **What Viola says to Orsino**

Ask students to prepare what Viola says to Orsino on her return to his palace.

## Focus on late 17th-century drama: Aphra Behn

Aphra Behn was a novelist, playwright, and translator, and is considered one of the first female professional writers. She was born in England in 1640. Reportedly – though it is not reliably confirmed – she grew up in Surinam in the Dutch West Indies, where she set her first novel, *Oroonoko*. Little is known of her early life, but she was probably a spy for the government of Charles II.

Her play *The Lucky Chance* was written in 1686. The play is an attack on the system, common at the time, whereby parents arranged for their daughters to marry much older men for money. In the extract, we meet Gayman, a spendthrift young man who is in love with a young woman, Julia, who has been married off to an old rich man. Eventually Julia becomes free and Gayman manages to marry her – and inherit a fortune as well.

Here, however, we present an early part of the play when Gayman is poor and is trying to deal with his angry landlady to whom he owes money. We have chosen it because it is lively and accessible, and gives rise to a number of different activities, including an activity on insults which can show that literature isn't only 'elevated language' but reflects everyday life.

### Teaching *The Lucky Chance*

As a pre-reading activity, get students to work in small groups and act one of the following role-plays.

- A landlord/landlady demands payment from a tenant who requests more time to find the money.
- A debt collector demands payment from a debtor who needs more time to find the money.
- A servant feels they deserve to be paid more by their master/mistress.

Then read through the extract and ask students to match the sentence equivalents in modern English below to the relevant parts of the extract. (They are in the same order as in the extract.)

---

*Gayman, a former soldier, now rake and fortune-seeker, and his servant, Rag, enter. Gayman is wearing an old campaign or army coat.*

| | |
|---|---|
| **Gayman** | How now, Rag, what's a clock? |
| **Rag** | My belly can inform you better than my tongue. |
| **Gayman** | Why, you gormandizing vermin, you, what have you done with the three pence I gave you a fortnight ago? |
| **Rag** | Alas, sir, that's all gone long since. |
| **Gayman** | You rascal, you are enough to breed a famine in a land. I have known some industrious footmen that have not only gotten their own livings, but a pretty livelihood for their masters too. |
| **Rag** | Aye, till they came to the gallows, sir. |

*Gayman's landlady enters*

| | |
|---|---|
| **Gayman** | A chair there for my landlady. |

---

| | |
|---|---|
| **Rag** | Here's ne're a one, sir. |
| **Landlady** | More of your money and less of your civility, good Sir. |
| **Gayman** | Dear Landlady … |
| **Landlady** | Dear me no dears, sir, but let me have my money – eight weeks rent last Friday; besides taverns, alehouses, chandlers, laundresses' scores, and ready money out of my purse; you know it, sir. |

TEXT 7.2     *Extract from* The Lucky Chance *(1686) by Aphra Behn*

### Modern English equivalents

1  What's the time? (**Answer:** *what's a clock?*)

2  It's past dinner-time and I'm hungry.
   (**Answer:** *My belly can inform you better than my tongue.*)

3  What's happened to the money I gave you two weeks' ago?
   (**Answer:** *what have you done with the three pence I gave you a fortnight ago?*)

4  You'd eat all the food that's available.
   (**Answer:** *you are enough to breed a famine in a land*)

5  I'd like more money from you and not so many fine words.
   (**Answer:** *More of your money and less of your civility*)

6  Don't call me 'dear'. (**Answer:** *Dear me no dears*)

---

**Try this** ☞  **Insults**

There are several colourful insults and exclamations in this extract. We have added some more to the list below from plays by Shakespeare. Ask students to try to work out their meaning. Which ones do they like? What is the function of the insults in the play?

1  You rascal (*The Lucky Chance*)
2  You gormandizing vermin (*The Lucky Chance*)
3  Away, you mouldy rogue, away! (*Henry IV Part II*)
4  I do desire we may be better strangers (*As You Like It*)
5  O thou vile one (*Cymbeline*)
6  Out, dunghill! (*King John*)
7  There's no more faith in thee than in a stewed prune (*Henry IV Part II*)
8  Thou whoreson zed, thou unnecessary letter! (*King Lear*)
9  You blocks, you stones, you worse than senseless things! (*Julius Caesar*)

---

**Try this** ☞  **Women playwrights**

1  With students, brainstorm the names of women novelists (in L1 and in English).
2  Now brainstorm the names of women poets (in L1 and in English)
3  Finally, brainstorm the names of women playwrights (in L1 and in English).

What conclusions do you reach? Extend the activity by discussing the comparable lack of women playwrights (as opposed to novelists or poets). Ask students to suggest reasons or do some research as to why this is the case. (Tell them to search online with the question: Why are there so few women playwrights?)

**Advert for a servant**

Ask students to imagine that Rag has left Gayman's employment and Gayman is now looking for a new servant. Students then write the advert that he would put in a newspaper.

## Focus on late 19th-century drama: Oscar Wilde

Oscar Wilde was born in Ireland. He was educated at Oxford University and then moved to London, where he dazzled society with his witty plays, poems, essays, short stories, and one novel, *The Picture of Dorian Gray*. He spent two years as an inmate of Reading prison, an experience which was the basis of his long poem, *The Ballad of Reading Gaol*. After his release he went to Paris, where he died two years later.

### Teaching *The Importance of Being Earnest*

*The Importance of Being Earnest* was first performed in 1895 and published in 1899. It is a witty and farcical comedy. Text 7.3 presents a scene between two of the main characters, Mr John Worthing and Miss Gwendolen Fairfax. Mr Worthing has a secret: he has two names and two identities. As he says earlier in the play, 'My name is Ernest in town and Jack in the country'. Gwendolen knows him as Ernest. The name gives rise to the double meaning of the title, which refers both to the meaning of 'earnest' as 'honest, reliable', and to the name Ernest. At the end of the play, we learn that Mr Worthing – who was abandoned as a baby – had actually been christened Ernest after all.

However, at this point in the play we do not know this. Part of the humour lies in the audience's knowledge that Ernest's name is in fact Jack – a name which Gwendolen dislikes: as she notes, it is a common family version of the name John.

There are several film versions of the play, which you could use together with the extract (see Chapter 8 for ideas).

| | |
|---|---|
| **Jack** | Charming day it has been, Miss Fairfax. |
| **Gwendolen** | Pray don't talk to me about the weather, Mr Worthing. Whenever people talk to me about the weather, I always feel quite certain that they mean something else. And that makes me so nervous. |
| **Jack** | I do mean something else. |
| **Gwendolen** | I thought so. In fact, I am never wrong. |
| **Jack** | And I would like to be allowed to take advantage of Lady Bracknell's temporary absence – |
| **Gwendolen** | I would certainly advise you to do so. Mamma has a way of coming back suddenly into a room that I have often had to speak to her about. |
| **Jack** | Miss Fairfax, ever since I met you I have admired you more than any girl – I have ever met since – I met you. |

| | |
|---|---|
| **Gwendolen** | Yes, I am quite aware of the fact. And I often wish that in public, at any rate, you had been more demonstrative. For me you have always had an irresistible fascination. Even before I met you I was far from indifferent to you. We live, as I hope you know, Mr Worthing, in an age of ideals. The fact is constantly mentioned in the more expensive monthly magazines … and my ideal has always been to love some one of the name of Ernest. There is something in that name that inspires absolute confidence. The moment Algernon first mentioned to me that he had a friend called Ernest, I knew I was destined to love you. |
| **Jack** | You really love me, Gwendolen? |
| **Gwendolen** | Passionately! |
| **Jack** | Darling! You don't know how happy you've made me. |
| **Gwendolen** | My own Ernest! |
| **Jack** | But you don't mean to say that you couldn't love me if my name wasn't Ernest? |
| **Gwendolen** | But your name is Ernest. |
| **Jack** | Yes, I know it is. But supposing it was something else? Do you mean to say you couldn't love me then? |
| **Gwendolen** | Ah! […] The only really safe name is Ernest. |
| **Jack** | Gwendolen, I must get christened at once – I mean we must get married at once. There is no time to be lost. |
| **Gwendolen** | Married, Mr Worthing? |
| **Jack** | Well – surely. You know that I love you, and you led me to believe, Miss Fairfax, that you were not absolutely indifferent to me. |
| **Gwendolen** | I adore you. But you haven't proposed to me yet. Nothing has been said at all about marriage. The subject has not even been touched on. |
| **Jack** | Well – may I propose to you now? |
| **Gwendolen** | I think it would be an admirable opportunity. And to spare you any possible disappointment, Mr Worthing, I think it only fair to tell you quite frankly beforehand that I am fully determined to accept you. |
| **Jack** | Gwendolen! |
| **Gwendolen** | Yes, Mr Worthing, what have you got to say to me? |
| **Jack** | You know what I have got to say to you. |
| **Gwendolen** | Yes, but you don't say it. |
| **Jack** | Gwendolen, will you marry me? (Goes on his knees.) |
| **Gwendolen** | Of course I will, darling. How long you have been about it! I am afraid you have had very little experience in how to propose. |
| **Jack** | My own one, I have never loved anyone in the world but you. |

TEXT 7.3    *Extract from* The Importance of Being Earnest *(1895) by Oscar Wilde*

During the course of the scene, Mr Worthing and Miss Fairfax address each other in several different ways, moving back and forth from more to less formal. Ask students to highlight or underline all the instances of these terms in the text.

| Mr Worthing addresses Miss Fairfax | Miss Fairfax addresses Mr Worthing |
| --- | --- |
| Miss Fairfax | Mr Worthing |
| Gwendolen | Ernest |
| Darling | Darling |
| My own one | My own Ernest |

TABLE 7.1  *Terms of address in extract from* The Importance of Being Earnest

In pairs or small groups, students should try to work out why each term is used when it is. What changes of feeling are indicated by the constant changes of term? A key factor is protocol: the more formal terms are used when the protocol of a marriage proposal needs to be observed.

A key strand in *The Importance of Being Earnest* is the meanings and emotions attached to the choice of personal names. In many cultures, someone's personal name is indeed their first name, but in other cultures the family name is presented first, followed by the personal name. In general, this is an interesting area of background knowledge to explore with learners (see Chapter 3 for other issues of background knowledge).

Ask students individually to reflect on their own personal name. Do they like it? Do they know why their parents chose it? Is there another name which they would prefer? Have they got a nickname? They can share their responses in pairs or groups. See if there are any points which pairs are willing to share with the whole class. Are there any generalisations emerging about the way people in the class are named?

**Try this** ☞ **Naming conventions and traditions**

Ask the class to find out if anyone knows someone:
- who is named after a grandparent, aunt, or uncle.
- who is named after a singer/film star who was famous when they were born.
- whose first name is their mother's family name.
- who was named because the first-born boy/girl in the family always has this name.
- whose name is the place where their parents met or had their honeymoon or a holiday.
- whose parents just thought the name suited them.

**Try this** ☞ **Conventions for marriage proposals**

There are many different conventions or protocols for marriage proposals in different cultures around the world and over time. Here is a list of the ones which are mentioned in the play:
1  The man must go down on his knees.
2  The man must actually say 'Will you marry me?'
3  It's best if the couple are alone.
4  It's helpful if the couple have already indicated their attraction to each other.

5   The woman should appear surprised when the man proposes.

6   Proposals should be genuine, that is not just for fun or for practice.

Ask students, in groups, to identify references to these points in the play. Which of the conventions are followed in the extract? Which are just alluded to? Which are flouted (or ignored or challenged)? Ask students to add other conventions from their own cultures.

# Focus on 20th-century drama: Athol Fugard

Athol Fugard is an award-winning South African playwright, novelist, actor and director, born in 1932.

His play *Blood Knot* was first performed in 1961, well before the abolition of apartheid. The play is, in effect, an attack on apartheid, and was closed down after just one performance; it has been performed many times elsewhere in the world since. It has just two characters, half-brothers, who share a one-room shack in the non-white part of the town of Port Elizabeth. In the scene of the extract, they remember one of their childhood games, which was to pretend that they were in a car, driving out in the countryside. It's very lively and tinged with nostalgia.

The name of the play derives from a knot that is tied in a rope used as a whip, and intended to draw blood, and serves as a metaphor for the play. The two half-brothers are blood relatives and tied together in mutual poverty and dependence. They both support but also irritate and even enrage each other.

## Teaching *Blood Knot*

In groups, tell students to study the following traditional sayings, which either appear in the extract or are suggested by its content. Ask what they mean in general, and what they mean to each student in particular.

• Make hay while the sun shines.
• Those were the days.
• Go to hell and back.
• Where do the good times go?

Can students imagine a situation when they would say these phrases? What feeling do they express? Discuss with students the feeling of nostalgia, the feeling that things were better once, or that the good times have gone away.

Next, ask students to try to recall any imaginary or make-believe games that they played as children. Can they tell them to classmates? They can quiz each other with the following questions:

• Who was involved in the game?
• What exactly was the game?
• What was the outcome? Is the memory a good or a bad one?

They could also try to write their memories of the game or imagine meeting someone they played the game with and having a conversation about it with them.

The following terms related to cars occur in the extract. Which of them do students know? In groups, ask them to compare their answers and check them in the dictionary, if necessary.

| toot-toot | tyres | bonnet | boot | wires | Chevy |
| windscreen | wheel | gear | brakes | doing 34, 80, etc. | |

You can either provide a diagram of a car and ask the group to label it, or ask the group to draw and label one themselves.

**Why this works** ▶

**Different types of preparation**

These three activities are each classic pre-reading activities. The first provides language preparation (because it includes phrases and sayings from the text) and also prepares the ground for a discussion of nostalgia, an important element in the extract. The second activity further prepares the ground by asking learners to think about situations that are very similar to the situation in the text. The third activity looks at some of the more specialized vocabulary of the text.

✓ **Getting it right**

**Gauging the amount of preparation**

If you feel students need a great deal of pre-reading preparation, do all three activities above. If, on the other hand, you feel that your students need little preparation either linguistically or conceptually, introduce the extract simply by saying: *We have all played role-play games. The extract we are going to read shows two brothers playing a memory game.*

Ask students to read the text and act it in pairs. Because the game that the brothers play is in the mind (and consequently doesn't require any props), the extract is particularly good for acting. Even if you don't ask students to do this at the very start of their experience of the text, make sure that at some point you do ask them to act it so that they appreciate the feeling of the extract and the relationship between the brothers.

| | |
|---|---|
| **Morris** | … How about the games we played? Think, Zach. Think carefully! There was one special one. Just me and you. I'll give you a clue. Toot-toot. Toot-toot. |
| **Zachariah** | (*thinking*) Wasn't there an old car? |
| **Morris** | Where would it be? |
| **Zachariah** | Rusting by the side of the road. |
| **Morris** | Could it be the ruins of an old Chevy, Zach? |
| **Zachariah** | Yes, it could. |
| **Morris** | And can we say without tyres and wires and things? |
| **Zachariah** | We may. |
| **Morris** | … and all the glass blown away by the wind? |
| **Zachariah** | Dusty. |
| **Morris** | Deserted. |
| **Zachariah** | Sting bees on the bonnet. |
| **Morris** | Webs in the windscreen. |
| **Zachariah** | Nothing in the boot. |
| **Morris** | And us? |
| **Zachariah** | In it. |
| **Morris** | We are? How? |

| | |
|---|---|
| **Zachariah** | Side by side. |
| **Morris** | Like this? |
| | *(He sits beside Zachariah.)* |
| **Zachariah** | Uh-huh. |
| **Morris** | Doing what? |
| **Zachariah** | Staring. |
| **Morris** | Not both of us! |
| **Zachariah** | Me at the wheel, you at the window. |
| **Morris** | Okay. Now what? |
| **Zachariah** | Now, I got this gear here and I'm going to go. |
| **Morris** | Where? |
| **Zachariah** | To hell and gone, and we aren't coming back. |
| **Morris** | What will I do while you drive? |
| **Zachariah** | You must tell me what we pass. Are you ready? Here we go! |
| | *(Zachariah goes through the motion of driving a car. Morris looks eagerly out of the window.)* |
| **Morris** | We're slipping through the streets, passing houses and people on the pavements who are quite friendly and wave as we drive by. It's a fine, sunny sort of day. What are we doing? |
| **Zachariah** | Twenty-four. |
| **Morris** | Do you see that bus ahead of us? |
| | *(They lean over to one side as Zachariah swings the wheel. Morris looks back.)* |
| | Chock-a-block with early morning workers. Shame. And what about those children over there, going to school? Shame again. On such a nice day. What are we doing? |
| **Zachariah** | Thirty-four. |
| **Morris** | That means we're coming to open country. The houses have given way to patches of green and animals and not so many people anymore. But they still wave … with their spades. |
| **Zachariah** | Fifty. |
| **Morris** | You're going quite fast. You've killed a cat, flattened a frog, frightened a dog … who jumped! |

[…]

| | |
|---|---|
| **Morris** | We played our games, Zach. |
| **Zachariah** | And now? |
| **Morris** | See for yourself, Zach. Here we are, later, and now there is Ethel as well and that makes me frightened. |
| **Zachariah** | Sounds like another game. |
| **Morris** | Yes … but not ours this time. Hell, man, I often wonder. |
| **Zachariah** | Same here. |
| **Morris** | I mean, where do they go, the good times, in a man's life? |
| **Zachariah** | And the bad ones? |
| **Morris** | That's a thought. Where do they come from? |
| **Zachariah** | Oudtshoorn.* |

* Oudtshoorn: town in the Western Cape province of South Africa

TEXT 7.4    *Extract from* Blood Knot *(1961) by Athol Fugard*

**Try this** ☞ **Video backdrop**

In many theatre productions the director incorporates a video backdrop that is projected behind the actors during the play. Ask students to write a paragraph describing what the video backdrop could be in this scene. They could either write it in the way someone would pitch an idea to a director, or prepare a storyboard (a series of sketches showing what would be filmed). They could also film their ideas on their mobile phones.

Discuss with students the relationship between the two brothers. Ask if it is it a good relationship. Are the brothers equal? Who is more educated? Who is likely to have a menial job? Who drives the conversation and the game? Does this change? Is this consistent?

Once you have discussed this, ask students to examine the extract carefully, and to provide actual evidence for their views by finding out which brother talks more (both in terms of the total number of words and the length of each turn), which one directs the game and what types of questions they each ask (e.g. directive, informational, etc.). You could also ask which of the brothers students like more, and ask them to justify their choices. This is particularly interesting in the light of how the play develops and how the brothers' relationship changes.

**Why this works** ⫸

> **Deepening understanding of character**
>
> This extract is interesting because, in spite of its simplicity, it reveals a lot about the two brothers and their relationship. Throughout the play, the two brothers are jostling for precedence, both celebrating their 'blood knot' and resenting it.

## Focus on 21st century drama: Timberlake Wertenbaker

Timberlake Wertenbaker was born in the USA in 1946 and educated in France. She now lives and works in Britain. She is an award-winning playwright, screenplay writer, and translator.

Her play *The Ash Girl*, first staged in 2000, presents a version of the Cinderella story. In it, Wertenbaker explores aspects of Cinderella's psychology, especially her tendency to sadness and her apparent willingness to accept her situation as an outcast: poor, friendless, abandoned by her father, and unloved by her step-mother and step-sisters. The play ends happily, as does the fairy story, with Cinderella marrying the Prince for love.

Try as many or as few of the pre-reading tasks below as you wish. Because the Cinderella story is so well known internationally, the shock of the way in which Wertenbaker subverts the story can be experienced by a class with very little preparation. Alternatively, you may feel that linguistically the class needs more preparation and construct some activities to help them with this.

## Teaching *The Ash Girl*

First, ask students to research the Cinderella story online. Tell them that there are a number of different versions and that they should find at least three different ones. They can then share the stories they have found in groups or as a whole class.

Next, ask students in groups to discuss how they would prepare for a ball or grand party. They might meet someone special there! All of their family (parents, siblings) will be going too. What will they wear? How will they behave?

Finally, ask students to fill in Table 7.2 with the brief descriptions below. They can add others, and then discuss their answers.

| Character | Attributes |
|---|---|
| Cinderella | |
| Father | |
| Step-mother | |
| Step-sisters | |
| Prince | |

TABLE 7.2  *Characters and attributes in* The Ash Girl

| | |
|---|---|
| is absent or ineffectual | is harsh and unloving |
| lives in the kitchen | is unfriendly to Cinderella |
| is poor | is treated as a servant |
| is handsome and rich | is greedy |
| is ugly | is beautiful |
| loves Cinderella | doesn't work |

Discuss some of the following questions in relation to the version(s) of Cinderella that students have brought in.

### Questions
- Where does the story take place? When?
- What are the stereotypes that the story builds on?
- Does the Cinderella story have any relevance for today?

Now ask students to study the extracts from *The Ash Girl*. Note that much of the dialogue consists of short utterances, which are not always full sentences. It may also be useful to be aware that Cinderella/Ashgirl first appears in Scene 2. She is, in fact, present in Scene 1, but hidden in the fireplace, covered in leaves and ashes. Gradually she emerges, and explains something of her background.

**Scene Two. Who Lives in the Ashes**

**Ashgirl** I don't remember much. It was another countryside, another country. Flowers inside. My mother loved flowers.

I don't know when she died, if she died. I was always with my father. I am your friend for ever, he said. He took me everywhere, travels, hunting, I sat under castle tables and listened to the men talk. We slept on his cloak in the woods, naming the stars.

Until we came here. First for an afternoon, then a night, then days, and finally to stay. He never told me he wanted to marry her, he didn't even ask me, his friend. And that these girls would be his daughters, call themselves my sisters. He said he loved me most, but he needed, needed – but he loved me.

He wasn't happy long. I saw lines of loneliness return to his face. I went to him, but he was strange. He told me he was not a good man, he had monsters to fight. I said I would fight them with him, but he said, no, these monsters were different, they'd poisoned the blood to his heart and I must forgive him. And so my father went in search of his heart and broke mine.

And that's when I found the ashes. Ashes are warm and in the ashes no one sees you, you do no wrong. Ashes on your head, no one talks to you, ashes on your arms, no one touches you, ashes are safe. I will stay in these ashes, melt into them, shrink to their weightlessness. Cloak of crumbling grey. My ashes.

TEXT 7.5    *Scene 2 of* The Ash Girl *(2000) by Timberlake Wertenbaker*

There is plenty of language repetition in Scene 2, both of words and of grammatical patterns, creating a highly poetic effect (particularly the last paragraph). Ask students to identify the repetitions and discuss their effect. You could also ask them to identify the way in which the monologue subverts the traditional Cinderella story and changes it. Asking them to keep a log of instances in which the fairy story continues to be subverted in subsequent extracts is also a useful activity.

> **Scene Three. Who Goes to the Ball**
>
> *The Mother comes in. She is held back, neat, straight. The girls follow her. She holds a large golden scroll in her hand.*
>
> **Mother**    I hoped it was from my husband, gifts, money. It's an invitation – addressed to all the daughters of the house.
>
> **Judith/Ruth**  We are the daughters of the house.
>
> **Ruth**    We haven't been anywhere all winter.
>
> **Mother**    You mustn't be seen with the wrong people.
>
> **Judith**    What are wrong people?
>
> **Mother**    When there's no father, people talk.
>
> **Ruth**    Let me read it.
>
> **Mother**    It's addressed to all the daughters of the house.
> *(She makes a gesture towards the ashes.)*
>
> **Ruth**    I am the oldest.
>
> **Judith**    But I am clever.
> *They both snatch at the scroll.*
>
> **Mother**    You can have a look too, Ashgirl.
>
> **Ashgirl**    *(from the ashes)* I'm not interested.
>
> **Mother**    It is to all my daughters.
>
> **Ashgirl**    *(emerging from the ashes)* I'm not your daughter!
>
> **Mother**    Clean yourself up. You look disgusting. You've got crumbs all over your face.
>
> **Ashgirl**    I'll clear the breakfast.
>
> **Mother**    Judith and Ruth can help you.
>
> **Ashgirl**    I like to do it myself.
>
> **Mother**    You don't help yourself, Ashgirl. I've heard people whispering I'm not nice to you, but I try.

TEXT 7.6    *Extract from Scene 3 of* The Ash Girl *(2000) by Timberlake Wertenbaker*

There are a number of expressions in this extract from Scene 3 that present stereotypical views of society: phrases such as 'the daughters of the house'; 'we haven't been anywhere all winter'; 'the wrong people'; 'where there is no father, people talk'. These expressions also suggest that the mother and her two daughters feel excluded from society. This is connected to the way in which the play subverts the traditional story.

Other expressions highlight the relationships between the characters: there is competition between the two daughters (one is older, the other cleverer). Ashgirl insists to the mother, 'I'm not your daughter'. Ask students to find these expressions.

**Try this** ☞  **Who speaks which line?**

Some extracts lend themselves well to presenting to the class without an indication of which line belongs to which character. You can do that at a later stage in the play, when learners should be able to identify more accurately (rather than just guess) which character speaks which line.

**Why this works** ⫸

> **Subverting expectations**
>
> The activities mentioned above make learners conscious of the way in which the play subverts the traditional story. They also highlight different assumptions underlying common everyday phrases, and sensitize learners to the use of language.

The extracts studied in this chapter span four centuries and different social classes. All of them, however, essentially explore the difficulties of human communication and the problems of reconciling individual desires with the needs of family and society. If you have studied more than one extract, ask learners to consider which one they prefer and which one they feel is most relevant to today's world.

**Part 3**     Working with related genres

# 8    Literature and film

For many learners, film is a more accessible medium than print, and many of the narratives that they know will have been experienced through film. Because films are such an important part of popular culture, using them in the classroom can help to promote an understanding of literature and also help learners bridge any perceived gap that they feel between the two.

The main reason you will probably show a film when using literature is to enhance appreciation of the literary work. A film provides the possibility of presenting a specific interpretation of the work, and where more than one version exists, you can illustrate different interpretations. A film also allows learners to gain a view of the piece as a whole. Films introduce variety into the classroom, and can help focus on important aspects of a play or novel. Their immediacy and learners' familiarity with them can be extremely helpful in sparking off discussions about the parallel literary work. Films also allow you to work on **visual literacy** or critical viewing as well as on non-verbal communication and cinematographic aspects such as camera work, set, props, soundtrack, or acting. Finally, because films are so accessible to learners, they are ideal for homework tasks – from short, focused viewing tasks to longer, creative tasks where learners create their own filmed reactions to the work that they are studying.

**Try this**  **Adapting reading activities**

Adapt some of the activities about reading literature in Chapters 1 and 2 to films. For example, *Find someone who* on pages 28–29, as well as *What makes you read* on page 29 are quite easily adapted.

✓ *Getting it right*    **When to watch**

At what point in the teaching and learning cycle should a film be used when studying a literary work? There are three likely approaches:

1   Before reading the book. This can be very helpful if you are reading a complex and more difficult text. It can draw learners in and motivate them to read: when they come to the reading they can focus on detail more easily since they know the plot, something about the characters, and they have already had an emotional response to the work.

2   After reading the book. If the reading has taken a long time and you have looked at various aspects of the work in detail, this is a way of stepping back and experiencing the work as a whole. It can then spark off a discussion of the differences between the film and the book, and can highlight the different ways in which film and literature achieve their effects.

3 Intermittently in the teaching cycle. For example, you can use the title sequence (see below) to introduce the work; then spend some time on the first few chapters and watch another segment of the film. This enables you to tailor specific activities to specific parts of the film and of the literary work.

✓ *Getting it right*

**What to watch**

It's probably most practical to use short film clips for intensive viewing and work in class. Sometimes, however, you will want learners to watch longer stretches for extensive viewing, and may not want to spend class time on watching the film. In such cases, learners can watch the film at home – on their own or in small groups. Either lend them your copy or ask them to stream or download it from a legal website. Importantly, watching extensively can contribute to the sense of enjoyment that learners get from the film.

## Working with the title sequence

The title sequence appears at the very beginning of any film and provides some of the important information about the film: the title, the main actors, the director, etc. A good title sequence can set the mood for the film, provide the background for the action, initiate the action, and predict some of the themes. All of these can become the focus of classroom activities.

### Using the title sequence before reading the work

An excellent example of this is the title sequence of the 1987 American Playhouse film of Arthur Miller's *All My Sons*, which portrays the events leading to the opening scene of the play. The sequence is only 1 minute 23 seconds long, and shows the branches and leaves of a tree during a storm. Slowly, the tree breaks and falls to the ground, and the sound of the wind on the soundtrack is replaced by a haunting phrase played on a muted trumpet. The action of the film then starts with one of the characters standing next to the tree, and the first line refers to the storm.

This title sequence can be used effectively with learners to predict what the film will be about. A quick question and answer session can elicit a great deal from learners. Questions could move from the general (What do you think the film is going to be about?), to more specific (What do you see in the sequence? What do you hear?), to more probing questions (What does a tree normally symbolise? What would a broken tree symbolize?).

**Try this** ☞ **Most recent title sequence**

Ask students, in groups, to think about the most recent film they have seen – either at home or in the cinema. Do they remember the title sequence? How did it work? Ask them to list the elements of title sequences in general.

**Try this** ☞ **Famous title sequences**

Choose some famous title sequences from the websites on page 140. Show them to students and elicit what the effect of each title sequence is and how it achieves it. For example, with the title sequence of *The Shining* (based on the novel by Stephen King), you could focus on the role of the music in creating suspense, the isolation of the location, and the feelings of threat and vulnerability created by the long shots of the car driving along the road.

**Try this** ☞ **Matching synopses to title sequences**

Provide students with synopses of five different novels or plays that have been filmed. Do not give them the names of the works or the films. Show them the title sequences for the five pieces and ask them to match the sequence to the synopsis.

**Try this** ☞ **Title sequence with sound off/on**

Show a title sequence with the sound off. Ask students to imagine the music that will be played at the same time. If the title sequence includes people speaking, you can also ask students to think of what words they might be saying, and write it down. Then play the sequence with the sound on, and compare students' suggestions with the actual music or dialogue.

**Try this** ☞ **Design a title sequence**

Ask students to design the title sequence for a film of the work you are studying. Ask them to think about:
- Period and setting
- Characters
- Soundtrack
- Use of stills
- Credits.

**Why this works** ⫸ | **Exploring the complexity of title sequences**

Thinking about the title sequence helps learners understand how it is part of the film and fulfils many functions. Finding music for a title sequence heightens learners' awareness of music and the way in which it can be used to create a mood as well as expectations or suggestions in the minds of viewers. When asked to design whole sequences, learners become aware of the complexity that can be expected from title sequences, examining the multi-layered choice made by film-makers.

## Teaching the metalanguage of film

It is highly likely that learners will have watched a large number of films and TV programmes, and may also have made short videos of their own using mobile phones or other technology. They will probably already know some of the metalanguage for film techniques (e.g. close-up, flashback, zoom) but there may be other techniques whose names are unfamiliar (e.g. long shot, establishing shot, high-angle shot, panning). To enable learners to discuss films in more depth and to be able to understand how certain effects are achieved, it may help to teach the metalanguage of film techniques. (For additional resources on film metalanguage, see www.oup.com/elt/teacher/itc)

## Focus on adaptation

There is a huge number of adaptations of literary works, ranging from faithful transfers of plays to screen (e.g. *All My Sons* by Arthur Miller), to plays that have been added to and changed (e.g. the most famous version of *The Importance of Being Earnest* by Oscar Wilde changes a great deal of dialogue, moves parts of scenes around, and adds other scenes), to faithful adaptations of novels, to the use of the bare plot as the plot of the film (e.g. the film *Bridget Jones's Diary* uses the novel of the same name, which is itself a reinterpretation of *Pride and Prejudice* by Jane Austen).

Films of plays are likely to be much more faithful to the original version, simply because the time that has been allotted to the play is similar to that allotted to a film. In contrast, when a longer novel is turned into a film, there are going to be inevitable cuts and changes. The concept of being faithful to the literary work is an issue that is debated by many theorists of adaptation. What does 'faithful' mean? To the spirit, to the letter, or to the plot? This can become a focus for discussion with learners.

An interesting and highly accessible example of adaptation is the 1985 film of *A Room with a View* by EM Forster. One overview activity can be to compare the structure of the novel and its twenty chapters with the structure of the film. Are all the chapters represented in the film? The only chapter that is totally absent is Chapter 5; all other chapters are represented, although there are various changes to them. (Note also that sequences in this film are often announced with the chapter titles from the novel. This is an interesting illustration of the way in which the film makes its connections with the novel explicit.)

One famous adaptation which has cut a significant amount from the original novel is David Lean's 1946 film of *Great Expectations* by Charles Dickens. A number of characters are omitted, and some of the events in the novel are changed – most conspicuously, the ending. This can become a focus for discussion, possibly with the additional information that the current ending of the novel was not the original one.

## Comparing parallel scenes from a film and a novel

*A Room with a View* by EM Forster and the 1985 film of the same name, mentioned above, are a good source of activities for comparing a film and a novel.

If you ask learners to compare the opening chapter of the novel with the opening sequence of the film, they should be able to note the following changes:
• Whereas the first four pages of the book happen at the dinner table, in the film the discussion of the lack of a view takes place as Lucy and

Miss Bartlett are in their rooms, looking into the courtyard. Some of their discussion continues as they walk down the stairs to the dining room.

- In the book, the guests are seated at one table, in two rows. In the film, they are seated at different tables.
- In the book, the question mark which George draws on a piece of paper is seen by Miss Bartlett only, as she goes to bed. In the film, the question mark appears at the meal, and George forms one with his food, and shows it to Lucy; the question mark he has drawn in his room is on the back of a print.
- An episode which is reported in the book later on – Mr Emerson warning one of the guests not to drink lemonade – is shown in the film in the first sequence at the table.
- In the film, one of the Miss Allans reminisces about seeing cornflowers in a field; later she is shown with cornflowers in her hair.

Once learners have identified the differences, you could ask them to match each difference to one of the following possible reasons:
1  Films can show, whereas novels can only tell.
2  Films need to compress the action, compared with a novel.
3  Motifs that will appear later are highlighted early on and a number of times.

Another interesting scene to compare between the film and the novel of *A Room with a View* is the murder scene which Lucy witnesses in Piazza della Signoria.

**Try this** ☞    **Adapting a scene for filming**

Choose a scene from a novel or a play that has been changed or abridged when adapted into a film. Give students the boundaries of the scene, and tell them how long it lasts in the film. Get them to adapt the scene for filming, with special attention to what will actually be spoken. Compare this with the actual film and discuss students' choices. Discuss what has been lost in the film version, and what has been gained.

## Understanding the use and effect of camera techniques

The 1985 film of *A Room with a View* is again a good source of activities for this aspect of adaptation. An interesting feature of the film is that many of the frames show two people at the same time: Lucy and Miss Bartlett; Mr Emerson and George Emerson; the two Miss Allans. You can elicit this from students by asking them to watch the first ten minutes of the film (after the title sequence) and asking them to note which kind of shot they notice is used most often.

Another interesting feature of the film is the regular use of establishing shots (or long shots) at the beginning of many sequences. Again, this is something that you may try to elicit from students. You can also try to elicit the effect that this has: for example, in the outdoor sequences, as well as the scenes inside the church of Santa Croce, this means that the viewer sees more of the Florentine setting.

Note some of the camera angles and shots with your students: for example, in the Santa Croce sequence, Mr Emerson asks Lucy to help George. The use of a low-angle shot (filming from below) when showing Lucy, and a high-angle shot (filming from above) when showing Mr Emerson makes Lucy appear more powerful in this context.

Another example you might want to explore is the way in which camera angles are used to great effect in the 1999 film of the novel *A Lesson Before Dying* by Ernest Gaines. It is set in the US state of Louisiana in the late 1940s; the difference in status between the members of the black community and the white community is repeatedly expressed through camera angles (e.g. by placing one of the white characters at the top of the stairs and using low-angle shots while he is speaking to a black character).

---

**Try this** ☞ **Effect of type of shot**

Find a scene with a very clear low-angle or high-angle shot. Ask students to read or reread the parallel section in the written version. Get them to think about how they would film this, considering the following questions:

1 What or who will the camera include in the shots?
2 Which type of shot will students use?
3 What camera angles will they use?
4 Will they include anything on the soundtrack in addition to the words being spoken?
5 How will the techniques they use convey the main ideas or atmosphere of the scene?

Now show students the sequence from the film, asking them to consider the following questions:

1 What is the effect of the way it is filmed? Why did the director choose to do this?
2 What has the scriptwriter omitted or changed? Why?
3 How has the director compensated for parts of the novel that were cut?

---

## Focus on acting

Films are also a good way of discussing acting with learners: it is possible to watch a scene and discuss the quality of the acting immediately, and then watch it again if there is disagreement about any aspect of the acting.

---

**Try this** ☞ **Use of gesture**

Choose a physical gesture or a non-linguistic form of communication that is repeated in one of the scenes in the film you are watching (e.g. smile, kiss, hug, laughter). Ask students to list the reasons why actors perform this gesture or sound. Watch the scene and decide what is meant in each case.

---

**Try this** ☞ **Use of props**

List the props that the actors use in a particular scene. Ask students why and how the actors use them. What is the effect? Is it symbolic?

---

A good way to focus on acting is to examine the way an actor delivers a monologue: this can be a soliloquy in a Shakespeare play, but equally a long turn in a modern play, for example, Joe Keller's description of how he returned from prison in *All My Sons*, or Amanda Wingfield's phone conversations in *The Glass Menagerie* by Tennessee Williams (where we hear only her side of the conversation).

In this extract from Shakespeare's *Macbeth* (Text 8.1), Macbeth, preparing for the final battle, learns that Lady Macbeth has died. The short soliloquy that follows is one of the most famous in Shakespeare's plays. It has provided the title for William Faulkner's novel, *The Sound and the Fury*, the title for Robert Frost's poem, *Out, out*, and probably many others. It makes use of one of Shakespeare's famous images of life as a play or a player.

| | |
|---|---|
| **Macbeth** | Wherefore was that cry? |
| **Seyton** | The queen, my lord, is dead. |
| **Macbeth** | She should have died hereafter; |
| | There would have been a time for such a word. |
| | Tomorrow, and tomorrow, and tomorrow, |
| | Creeps in this petty pace from day to day |
| | To the last syllable of recorded time, |
| | And all our yesterdays have lighted fools |
| | The way to dusty death. Out, out, brief candle! |
| | Life's but a walking shadow, a poor player |
| | That struts and frets his hour upon the stage |
| | And then is heard no more: it is a tale |
| | Told by an idiot, full of sound and fury, |
| | Signifying nothing. |

TEXT 8.1    *Extract from* Macbeth *(1606) by William Shakespeare*

---

**Try this** ☞    **Reading a monologue**

Ask students to read silently the monologue from *Macbeth* or a different monologue you have provided for them. They should not read it too fast; tell them to imagine they are reading it aloud in front of a class. Then ask them to mark the words they would stress, where they would pause, which phrases they would read fast and which they would most enjoy saying. Next, ask them to read the text aloud to their partner, taking turns. Finally, show them the speech they have read (in different film adaptations, if possible). In what way is the acting similar or different to what they wanted to do? What do they think of the actor in each case?

## Comparing film versions

Sometimes you may find that the work you are reading has many different cinematic versions. In such cases, you can compare the treatment of the same part of the work and discuss which cinematic version is more effective. Shakespeare's plays are particularly appropriate for this – *Macbeth*, for example, has been filmed a number of times. You could compare the following very different versions: 1948 (directed by and starring Orson Welles); 1971 (directed by Roman Polanski); 1978 (directed by Trevor Nunn); 2015 (directed by Justin Kurzel with Michael Fassbender in the lead role).

Each of these versions approaches the script in very different ways. Orson Welles's version makes a variety of changes to the play, and is a mixture of realism and abstract sets. Most importantly, it recasts many of the soliloquys as internal monologues using the technique of voice-over. Roman Polanski's film attempts to be realistic, down to the gory detail of Macbeth's head rolling on the battlefield after he is killed. Trevor Nunn's version retains the feeling of a theatre and the actors wear modern costume.

Looking at different cinematic versions of Shakespeare's plays is a good opportunity to understand different viewpoints of the same play. It is also a good opportunity to read different reactions to these film versions. Because not all the versions are successful, this is an opportunity to make learners more aware of what is successful and what is not; how different directors may approach the same text; and how critique and criticism can be expressed when discussing these versions. Learners can be shown how to go beyond simplistic expressions of liking or disliking, and teachers can incorporate elements of critical thinking into the classroom.

**Try this ☞** **Matching statements to clips**

Prepare six to ten statements characterising the different film versions that you are going to show to students. Some statements can refer to one version, some can refer to both. After watching the film clips, students decide which version each statement refers to. The statements can be either descriptive or critical, depending on the language level of students and on what you want to achieve with the activity.

# Using film websites

There are many websites which provide cast lists, synopses, and both professional and amateur reviews (see page 140). Many reviews of films provide a synopsis of the plot, a summary of the characters, and some general words about the feel of the film. Interestingly, very few reviews talk about the cinematic aspects of films or how they achieve their effects. This in itself can be an important point to make to learners, sensitizing them to the quality of reviews that they read.

**Try this ☞** **Respond to reviews**

Using the IMDb website or the Rotten Tomatoes website (see page 140), find several reviews of the film that you will be using with your class. Choose a number of very short extracts from these reviews to show students. Use the walkabout technique to elicit their responses, which they can then write down.

# 9  Literature, art, and music

## Literature and art

Literature and art have always interacted. Many writers have responded to paintings and sculptures in their work; likewise, many artists have responded to literature in paintings and sculptures. Many artists have illustrated poetry collections, novels, and plays either at the time when they were first published, or later on. In some cases, many different artists have provided illustrations for successive editions of the book, and some writers have illustrated their own books. An interesting recent phenomenon which embodies this interaction is the **graphic novel**, where illustrations and text both contribute to the experience of reading equally. This is rich material, especially for learners motivated by visual stimuli in a world where much of our communication is multimodal – that is, conducted through verbal channels, visual channels, the screen, and moving image.

In the past, a teacher who wanted to use paintings or photos in the classroom had to find books or postcards of these paintings and bring them to class. The internet has made this much easier, and you can now find high-quality digital images of paintings and project them in class.

There are many ways in which art can be used in language lessons in conjunction with literature. Very often, discussing a painting can take a whole lesson. Learners don't necessarily need to know that this will lead to a literary text – in many cases, a lesson on a piece of art can stand on its own, and you can make the link to the literature in the following lesson.

## Poems responding to works of art

In most cases, a poem responding to a painting will have been written with the assumption that the reader will be familiar with the painting. Since we can't assume that about learners, the best way to start is to construct an activity around the painting.

### Starting with describing

One way of starting is by asking learners to perform the basic task of describing a painting. For such tasks, learners will need both the vocabulary specific to the work they are describing, as well as some more general expressions for describing works of art. Obviously, the skills and language practised here will be useful in other contexts – for example, in exams which ask learners to discuss photos.

There are many ways of describing paintings; descriptions can be general, specific, focus on the mood and atmosphere, focus on the main event/scene, or focus on details. The type of description that you ask learners to do will depend on the poem (or story), its relationship to the painting, and what you would like your learners to do with the painting.

### Integrating responses to art and literature

One of the most famous poems written in response to a work of art is *Musée des Beaux Arts* by WH Auden, in which the poet reflects on the painting *Landscape with the Fall of Icarus* by Pieter Brueghel the Elder. The painting is in the Museum of Fine Arts in Brussels, which gives the poem its name.

First, ask students to look at the painting and to make a list of the actual things that they see.

FIGURE 9.1    Landscape with the Fall of Icarus *by Pieter Brueghel the Elder*

The lists are likely to include: ships, ploughman, horse, sea, sun, sheep, shepherd, town/city/village, rocks, etc. Learners may not know some of these words (e.g. ploughman or plough) so this is an opportunity to teach them; what this activity creates is a need on the part of learners to use these words. You can also do some pronunciation work (ship/sheep is an obvious one) as well as talk about British vs. American spelling (plough/plow).

Try to get students to make their descriptions as specific as possible; so when a group lists the ploughman, you can ask them what he is doing. The same goes for the shepherd – if you ask students to describe him in more detail, this may elicit (or you can introduce) expressions such as 'gazing up' and 'leaning on his stick/staff'. Answers to this activity are often naturally convergent, i.e. students usually come up with very similar lists.

✓ *Getting it right*

**List what you see**

When first looking at a painting, it is important for learners to list what they actually see, rather than describe the painting in general terms. This leads on more effectively to the next activity and also enables you to elicit the words needed to understand the poem or literary work.

Once students have made their lists, produce a joint list on the board. Ask them to tell you what they saw, in the order in which they saw it. At some point, a student will mention the legs in the bottom right-hand corner; some students think the legs belong to a swimmer or a diver, and some realize that this is a person drowning. This often provokes some discussion.

✓ *Getting it right*

**Describing paintings**

Asking learners to describe a variety of paintings may require you to phrase questions in a slightly different way. With some paintings, you may choose to ask learners to describe the feelings of the people in the painting rather than just list what they see. Every describing activity can be used to pre-teach expressions such as 'in the top/lower right/left-hand corner', 'in the foreground', 'perspective', 'the viewer', etc. Some paintings also include quite a lot of movement, so lend themselves to teaching prepositions or 'verb + preposition' combinations such as 'away from', 'towards', 'gaze up', 'fall down'.

Ask students to provide a title for the painting. Common suggestions usually focus on the countryside aspect of the painting and its calm atmosphere. After revealing the painting's real title, explain that the legs on the right belong to Icarus. Even if most students don't know the story of Icarus, it is enough if one or two remember bits of it, so you can elicit this from them and build up the story together.

At this point, you can bring in a written version of the story as told by Ovid in Book VIII of his *Metamorphoses* (see page 140 for an online source). Give the text to students, and ask them to skim through it quickly and to demonstrate to you that Brueghel knew it well. The clues are in the very specific descriptions, in the *Metamorphoses*, of the fisherman with his rod, the shepherd and his staff, and the ploughman bent over his plough. Point out that all three of these figures appear in the painting.

Now discuss with students the meaning of the painting and why Icarus is such a minor figure in it. It is normally possible to elicit from learners that this is a commentary on Brueghel's part that life goes on while tragedies happen.

**Try this** ☞ **Other paintings by Brueghel**

Bring in other paintings by Brueghel where momentous events happen but the painting seems to be mainly about everyday life (e.g. *The Numbering at Bethlehem* or *The Massacre of the Innocents*). You can also bring in paintings of the same themes by other painters (e.g. *The Massacre of the Innocents* by Tintoretto) to show how in other paintings the actual tragedy is usually more prominent.

**Why this works** ⫸

> **The importance of structuring activities**
>
> Everything in this highly structured lesson is a preparation for introducing the poem. It introduces the actual language needed to understand the poem, but most importantly, it also provides the essential background knowledge. By spending a long time on the background, learners will have thought about it, internalized it, and taken a position in relation to the issues that it raises. This is very different from simply showing learners the painting, telling them the story, and then immediately going into the poem.

At this point, introduce the poem by WH Auden (Text 9.1). Since the previous activities may well have taken up a whole lesson, you can introduce and read it briefly at the end of the lesson, and then come back to additional activities in the next lesson; alternatively, you can simply start the next lesson by showing the poem itself.

> **Musée de Beaux Arts**
>
> About suffering they were never wrong,
> The Old Masters: how well they understood
> Its human position; how it takes place
> While someone else is eating or opening a window or just walking
>     dully along;
> How, when the aged are reverently, passionately waiting
> For the miraculous birth, there always must be
> Children who did not specially want it to happen, skating
> On a pond at the edge of the wood:
> They never forgot
> That even the dreadful martyrdom must run its course
> Anyhow in a corner, some untidy spot
> Where the dogs go on with their doggy life and the torturer's horse
> Scratches its innocent behind on a tree.
>
> In Brueghel's Icarus, for instance: how everything turns away
> Quite leisurely from the disaster; the ploughman may
> Have heard the splash, the forsaken cry,
> But for him it was not an important failure; the sun shone
> As it had to on the white legs disappearing into the green
> Water; and the expensive delicate ship that must have seen
> Something amazing, a boy falling out of the sky,
> Had somewhere to get to and sailed calmly on.

TEXT 9.1    Musée de Beaux Arts *(1940) by WH Auden*

Read the poem to students at least once, and then discuss whether Auden accepts Brueghel's point of view (that disasters and daily events accompany each other as a fact of life) or whether he is protesting about this. We have found that teenagers often project their own views onto the poem, misreading it as a poem of protest against the injustice of the world. It may take some time to show them that the poem actually accepts the point of view which Brueghel expresses in the painting, although the first two lines indicate this quite clearly.

Try this ☞   **Anglo-Saxon vs. Latinate words**

Look at the words that Auden uses to describe each part of the paintings. Show students how the everyday actions are described mainly with short Anglo-Saxon words (e.g. 'window', 'dully'), whereas the extraordinary events are depicted using longer Latinate words (e.g. 'suffering', 'passionately'). What is the effect of this?

Try this ☞   **Other poems about the same painting or story**

Compare Auden's poem with William Carlos Williams' poem, *Landscape with the fall of Icarus*. The latter poem is even more detached than the one by Auden. There are also other poems which deal with the painting or the story (e.g. *Icarus Shmicarus* by Adrian Mitchell, *To a Friend Whose Work Has Come to Triumph* by Anne Sexton, and *Lines on Brueghel's Icarus* by Michael Hamburger).

Try this ☞   **Poem inspired by Auden**

Compare Auden's poem with that of Jeremy Kingston: *Musea voor Schone Kunsten* – the Flemish name of the same museum. Kingston uses a very similar structure to Auden, both in terms of the poetic structure (note the clear rhymes) and the structure of the argument, but he takes a very different stand.

---

**Musea voor Schone Kunsten**

About suffering they told bloody lies,
the Old Masters: oh, they could always paint
dogs scrapping in a corner while the saint
down in the foreground elegantly dies;
life carries on regardless: big surprise.
It's the main subject pushes my complaint,
the martyr's decorous, demure restraint
while spears jab, arrows ping and hot oil fries.

In Memling's *St Sebastian* note how
the languorous youth reclines against his tree;
though five times punctured, nothing's going to start
the faintest frown rippling along that brow:
sweet poses, prettifying sanctity,
turn crimes to candy in the name of art.

---

TEXT 9.2   Musea voor Schone Kunsten *(2008) by Jeremy Kingston*

**Try this ☞**   **Poems about sculptures**

There are fewer poems that respond to sculptures, and in many ways it is more difficult to discuss sculptures in the language classroom because there are usually fewer significant details. However, some poems that have responded to sculptures and which you might use are: *Giacometti's Dog* by Robert Wallace; *At the Tate*, by Dannie Abse; *Rodin's 'The Kiss'* by Ruth Silcock; *Rodin's Muse* by Alison Fell.

## Prose works responding to works of art

One particularly good example of a prose work responding to a work of art is Chapter 5 of *A History of the World in 10½ Chapters* (1989) by Julian Barnes. It is entitled 'Shipwreck', and focuses on the painting *The Raft of the Medusa* by the French painter, Théodore Géricault. The first section of the chapter tells the story of the frigate *Medusa*, which sank in 1816 off the shore of Africa, and of the 15 crew and passengers who survived (from a total of over 150) on a raft. The second section tells the story of how Géricault painted his famous painting, exhibited in 1818. It discusses the process of painting, details the different stages and sketches Géricault made, relates the painting to the actual events, and comments and discusses different ways of interpreting it. In advanced classes, particularly classes interested in art, you could try the following sequence of activities:

1   Ask students to describe what they see in Géricault's painting. How many men are there? What are they doing? Why are they waving? What questions does the painting raise?

2   Read Section 1 of 'Shipwreck'. Does it answer any of the questions raised in Step 1? Does it raise any other questions?

3   Read the first two and a half pages of Section 2. Does it answer any of the new questions from Step 2?

4   Read and discuss the rest of the chapter.

5   Compare the interpretations which Barnes presents with a more traditionally written interpretation (see page 140 for an online source).

6   Discuss the relevance of the image to our times – for example, the artist Kara Walker used the painting as a departure point for her 2007 cover of *The New Yorker* to commemorate the anniversary of Hurricane Katrina (see page 140 for an online source).

## Connecting literature, art, and other curriculum subjects

One of the benefits of using art in connection with literature is that it is an opportunity for cross-curricular learning. In the activities we discuss in this book, there are connections with history (in paintings and poems from WWI below), with the Bible (in the Wilfred Owen poem in Chapter 3), and with Greek mythology (in the WH Auden poem earlier in this chapter).

Artists have often responded to the same historical events in different works that have become an important part of the cultural heritage of a country. In such cases, it is possible to construct inter-disciplinary units that will bring in history, art, and literature. Many of these events are either foundational events (e.g. the birth of cities and countries or the discovery of continents) or wars.

**Try this** ☞ **WWI paintings**

Use paintings in conjunction with WWI poetry to introduce this specific conflict or wars in general. (See Useful websites on page 140.) One famous example is the painting *Gassed* by John Singer Sargent; others are *We Are Making a New World* by Paul Nash and *The Screened Road to A* by AY Jackson. The latter can serve as a good introduction to Isaac Rosenberg's poem *Returning, we hear the larks*, as both deal with life behind the trenches. The Imperial War Museum in London has a large collection of WWI paintings from Britain and other countries.

## Encouraging learners' artistic creativity

In earlier sections of this chapter we provided examples of literature written in response to art. We can also use the artistic impulses of learners and ask them to respond to literature. Some poems provide very vivid situations which are very clear, and which can be drawn fairly easily. The important thing to remember is that rather than testing their artistic ability, you are actually helping their comprehension and spoken fluency (when attempting to describe their interpretations).

**Try this** ☞ **Drawing a poem**

*Stopping by Woods on a Snowy Evening* by Robert Frost is a short poem. Its simple language and series of very concrete images make it highly accessible to learners at all levels, and most importantly to learners at a fairly low level of proficiency.

- Ask students to close their eyes. Tell them that you will read them a poem a number of times, and that you would like them to see in their mind's eye what is happening in the poem. Read the poem or play a recording of it.
- Ask them to draw the scene as they have imagined it.
- Ask them to share their finished drawings in pairs or in groups, and explain what they did and why.

**Try this** ☞ **Drawing a passage from a novel or short story**

Many novels and short stories have short, descriptive passages that lend themselves to a drawing activity. For example, the opening of Kate Chopin's *The Kiss* (see Chapter 4) is highly descriptive and could be used as an impetus for a drawing.

**Try this** ☞ **Which scene/chapter?**

Find a number of illustrations of the same novel or play and ask students to identify which scene/chapter they illustrate.

**Try this** ☞ **Crowd scene**

Find an illustration of a scene of a novel or play which has a crowd or large number of people in it (e.g. Thomas Stothard's picture of Act II, Scene I from *Othello*). Give students the list of characters in the illustration and ask them to label it.

**Try this** ☞ **One-sentence painting**

Ask students to choose one sentence from the short story you are studying that they think would make the best painting.

## Looking at graphic novels

Graphic novels integrate the verbal and the visual in unique ways, and require readers to read both the text and the pictorial text to achieve understanding. A good example of this genre is the 2009 version of Charles Dickens's *Great Expectations* by Jen Green et al.

FIGURE 9.2    *Page from graphic novel of* Great Expectations *(2009) by Jen Green et al*

There is much that can be learnt from the pictorial aspect of this page. The large panel on which the smaller panels are set serves a similar function as an establishing shot in a film (see Chapter 8). Although we don't see the marshes in which the opening of the novel is set, it is clear that the church is a lonely place; we wonder why the child is laying flowers at the grave. The letters 'RIP' on the gravestone can be explained. The most interesting panel is the middle-left one, where the reader becomes aware of the threat that Pip is under; interestingly, it is more threatening than the actual panels showing the convict Magwitch with Pip.

The different versions of *Great Expectations* – the full novel, the simplified novel, the graphic novel, and the ELT graphic novel – can be used together to provide differentiation in teaching. For example, different students can read different versions; although the graphic novel version lacks some of the reflective elements and Pip's commentary on his own story, it does provide a faithful rendering of the narrative. Another way of doing this would be to alternate between versions, for example, taking the graphic novel version and supplementing it with some of the reflective paragraphs from the novels.

**Try this** ☞    **Graphic novel vs. original novel**

Ask students to read the text of Dickens' original novel and note what has been included in the graphic novel version and what has not. (For the original opening passage, see additional resources on www.oup.com/elt/teacher/itc) Do they agree with the omissions? Taking into account space considerations, would they have made the same choice? Then ask them if there are any additional pictorial elements that they would add to the illustrations. For example, some students might want to add the detail from the novel of 'the five little stone lozenges, each about a foot and a half long', which represent the graves of Pip's siblings.

## Literature and music

In the same way as literature has been connected to art, it has also been connected to music. There are famous passages in novels describing characters' reactions to music – EM Forster's description of Lucy's playing in *A Room with a View* and of Helen reacting to Beethoven's 5th symphony in *Howards End* are two famous examples. Likewise, many musicians have set literary works to music, written incidental music to plays, or composed operas based on novels. Some poets have written libretti for operas, such as WH Auden and Chester Kalman's libretto for Stravinsky's opera *The Rake's Progress* (based on Hogarth's paintings), or Michael Symmons Roberts' libretto for James Macmillan's opera, *The Sacrifice*.

A productive example to work with is *Full Fathom Five*, the second verse of Ariel's song from Shakespeare's *The Tempest*.

> Full fathom five thy father lies;
> Of his bones are coral made;
> Those are pearls that were his eyes;
> Nothing of him that does fade
> But doth suffer a sea-change
> Into something rich and strange.
> Sea nymphs hourly ring his knell:
> Ding-dong,
> Hark! Now I hear them – Ding-dong, bell.

TEXT 9.3    *Extract from* The Tempest *(1611) by William Shakespeare*

Ask students which adjectives they would use to describe this song. How would they describe the attitude to death? Are there any other words (adjectives or nouns) that they would want to add from a list you could provide, for example, 'melancholy', 'comforting', 'disturbing', 'solemn', etc.?

Two settings of *Full Fathom Five* are available online (see page 141). After you have listened in class, ask students which version they prefer and why. You could also ask them to consider the following reactions of one listener to the different versions. Ask them which of the two versions the listener refers to in each case:

### Listeners' reactions

1 I've always wondered what in this particular text has drawn so many composers to set it to music. This setting provides a convincing answer – listening to it I can feel myself looking from the ocean bed upwards and seeing the reflection of the light in the water. There is wonderful 'word-painting' throughout the work. And yet, although I can feel I'm lying at the bottom of the sea, it's completely calm and peaceful.

2 This setting strikes me as odd. I can hear no connection to the words. It's too high (certainly for this particular singer), too noisy – in my opinion, it misses the point.

---

**Try this** ☞ **Present one piece of music**

Ask students to find as many pieces as they can of music inspired by the literary work they are studying, or settings of it. Ask them to present one of the pieces of music to their classmates and explain whether they like it or not, and why.

---

**Try this** ☞ **Musical settings of poems**

The poem *Stopping by Woods on a Snowy Evening* by Robert Frost has been set to music by different composers. Ask students to listen to two or more of them and say which one they prefer. Alternatively, prepare a number of written reactions to these musical settings and ask students to match the reactions to the setting. Other examples of musical settings of poems include Benjamin Britten's settings of poems by Blake, Tennyson, and others in his *Serenade for Tenor, Horn and Strings*.

# Glossary

**Aesthetic function**  See *poetic function*.

**Aesthetic reading**  Way of reading a text in which there is a focus on the personal, private experience and enjoyment of reading. It contrasts with *efferent reading*.

**Alliteration**  Sequence of words beginning with the same consonant, as in the first two lines of *The Eagle* by Alfred Lord Tennyson with the repetition of /k/: 'He <u>c</u>lasps the <u>c</u>rag with <u>c</u>rooked hands'.

**Assonance**  Occurrence of similar vowels in nearby words, normally in stressed syllables, for example, from *In Memoriam* by Alfred Lord Tennyson: 'the trees laid their d<u>ar</u>k <u>ar</u>ms about the field'.

**Canon**  Traditional list of great works of literature. In English this includes, amongst others, the works of William Shakespeare, Jane Austen, and Charles Dickens. Critics today challenge this list as being too UK-focused and class-based.

**Comedy**  Drama whose main purpose is to delight and entertain and which will end happily for most of the characters. It contrasts with tragedy, a type of drama which alarms but uplifts, and typically ends with the death of many of the characters.

**Directive function**  Where the aim of a piece of text is to direct or influence someone else's actions, through giving orders (e.g. 'Get out!') or making requests, (e.g. 'Please pass the salt').

**Discourse structure**  Sequence of actions as presented in a text, for example, 'I rushed out of the house, not having had time for breakfast and having got up only ten minutes earlier'. The event or typical, real-life structure (the *event structure*) which we can infer is 'Got up, missed breakfast, went out'.

**Efferent reading**  Way of reading in which there is a focus on information to be gleaned from the text. For a work of literature it would, for example, be reading in order to remember the plot (rather than being immersed in the plot, which would be an *aesthetic reading*).

**Entertainment function**  Where the aim of a piece of text is to entertain or give pleasure, for example, jokes, punning, nonsense prose or verse, and tongue-twisters (e.g. She sells seashells by the sea shore).

**Evaluation**  Possible element in the *Situation/Problem pattern* for *narrative* (e.g. 'It was terrible!', 'I was so scared.')

**Event structure**  Actual sequence of events in a situation, for example, 'Got up, washed and dressed, had breakfast, went to school.' It may be related in this sequence in a text, or the writer may choose a different sequence, or *discourse structure*, for a particular effect.

**Expressive function**  Where the aim of a piece of text is the expression of personal feeling (e.g. 'I hate green vegetables', 'I love you').

**Free verse**  Text which is written with line breaks, as poetry, but which has no overall pattern of *rhyme*, *rhythm*, or line length (e.g. *Musée des Beaux Arts* by WH Auden).

**Genre**  Type of text. Key and overarching literary genres are poetry, novels, short stories, and plays. There are many sub-genres, for example, novels can be romantic novels, detective novels, novels for young adults, etc.

**Graphic novel**  Text which is told through visuals, typically in a patterned sequence of boxes or frames and with speech bubbles. The term is not only used for works of fiction, but also for non-fiction works written in this way.

**Informational function**  Where the aim of a piece of text is to give factual information (e.g. It's Tuesday today).

**Interactional function**  Where the aim of a piece of text is to promote social contact. The text may well not convey any factual information, and may not even be entirely truthful (e.g. 'How are you?' 'Fine, thanks'). Also referred to by academics as *phatic function*.

**Intertextual reference**  Reference in one text to another text, for example, referring to the Bible or to Homeric heroes.

**Metalanguage**  Language used to talk about language itself. Now used also in a more general sense as language used to describe various systems (e.g. the metalanguage of film).

**Metalingual function** Where the aim of a piece of text is to comment on language itself, for example, when a teacher says to a student, 'You are using very vague terms.'

**Metaphorical** Where two disparate ideas or entities are presented as being the same, and transferring the features of one or both to the other. For example, 'My love is a red rose' equates the idea of a woman and a rose, implying that both are beautiful but both have problems (sharp thorns).

**Metre** Regular patterns of stressed and unstressed syllables in poems, sometimes referred to as *rhythm*. There are many metrical patterns in English poetry, depending on the number of syllables per word and the number of stresses per line of verse.

**Multimodal** Describes communication that incorporates linguistic elements together with other elements such as visual or spatial ones. For example, *graphic novels* are multimodal because they use pictures. The layout of texts and using space or gesture also provide clues to meaning, and are therefore multimodal.

**Narrative** Another term for 'story', i.e. a text which has a *plot*, happens through time, and is told by one person (a narrator) to another.

**Nonsense verse** Fantasy writing which combines absurd ideas, as found in the work of Edward Lear (e.g. his limericks) and in *Alice in Wonderland* by Lewis Carroll.

**Parallelism** Two or more lines of text, often in a poem, which have the same grammatical structure (e.g. noun + infinitive + noun) as in a text advertising tea as 'a tea to welcome the morning, a tea to soothe your midnights'.

**Phatic function** See *interactional function*.

**Plot** Core of a story or narrative which tells what happens, for example, 'the heroine is born, grows up poor, meets and rescues a frog from danger, discovers that the frog is actually a rich and handsome prince, and finally marries the prince'.

**Poetic function** Where the aim of a piece of text is to please the reader through the use of attractive-sounding words, including *rhyme* and *assonance*. Meaning is secondary. An example is from the song in *The Princess* by Alfred Lord Tennyson which repeats the line 'Blow, bugle, blow, set the wild echoes flying'.

**Poetic literacy** Familiarity with typical patterns and devices of poetry (e.g. rhyme schemes, *rhythm*, metaphor, etc.).

**Prose** Language which is not patterned in a regular way, in contrast with poetry.

**Protagonist** The leading character in a play, poem, novel or film, etc.

**Rhyme** Matching or echoing sounds at the ends of lines of poetry, as in the first two lines of *The Eagle* by Alfred Lord Tennyson: 'He clasps the crag with crooked hands; / Close to the sun in lonely lands'.

**Rhythm** More general word for *metre*, used in a non-technical sense.

**Set** Way the stage is arranged and furnished for a play.

**Situation/Problem pattern** Basic outline or typical *plot* summary for *narrative*, originally identified by the American sociolinguist, William Labov. For example, 'I was in a situation, a problem arose, I responded to the problem, I was successful/unsuccessful'.

**Stanza** Unit of several lines of poetry, often with an identifiable *rhyme* structure (e.g. a-b-a-b). This sub-division of a poem is also called a 'verse'.

**Subtext** Ideas or feelings not explicitly stated in a text but which the writer intends the reader to understand.

**Visual literacy** Understanding of the way in which visual texts convey their meaning, and an ability to discuss it using the appropriate *metalanguage* (e.g. 'foreground', 'background').

**Young adult (YA) literature** Texts, mainly novels, written especially for young people aged 13–19. The *protagonists* are often teenagers themselves, and the subject matter is the life of people their age.

# Useful websites

**Chapter 1**

Project Gutenberg:
Free e-books for out-of-copyright novels, plays, etc.
The search function will help you find the specific works you want:
www.gutenberg.org

**Chapter 2**

Poetry websites:
www.poets.org
www.poetrysociety.org.uk

Proverbs and quotes:
www.quotegarden.com
www.keepinspiring.me
en.proverbia.net
www.goodreads.com

Critical views of the poem *Richard Cory*:
www.english.illinois.edu/maps/poets/m_r/robinson/cory.htm

**Chapter 3**

Websites on Asperger's Syndrome to use in conjunction with *The Curious Incident of the Dog in the Night-Time* by Mark Haddon:
www.autism.org.uk/working-with/education/education-professionals-in-fe-and-he/college-and-university-supporting-students-with-asperger-syndrome.aspx
services.unimelb.edu.au/__data/assets/pdf_file/0006/688740/TowardsSuccessAspergers.pdf

**Chapter 5**

Robert Frost reading his own poem *Stopping by Woods on a Snowy Evening*:
www.youtube.com/watch?v=hfOxdZfo0gs

Two readings of the poem *Stopping by Woods on a Snowy Evening* by Robert Frost (with words on screen):
www.youtube.com/watch?v=wXo_bmftaEM

**Chapter 7**

Websites discussing women playwrights:
www.theguardian.com/stage/2012/dec/10/women-in-theatre-glass-ceiling
www.telegraph.co.uk/women/womens-life/10162258/Fewer-women-playwrights-A-professors-stats-just-dont-add-up.html

List of films based on Cinderella in different languages:
en.wikipedia.org/wiki/Category:Films_based_on_Cinderella

## Chapter 8

Film title sequences:
www.artofthetitle.com
www.creativebloq.com/design/top-movie-title-sequences-10121014

Ian McKellen in Trevor Nunn's TV version of Shakespeare's *Macbeth*:
www.youtube.com/watch?v=4LDdyafsR7g

Ian McKellen talking about the *Tomorrow, and tomorrow, and tomorrow* soliloquy from Shakespeare's *Macbeth*:
www.youtube.com/watch?v=zGbZCgHQ9m8

Film cast lists, synopses, trailers, etc.:
www.imdb.com

Professional and amateur film reviews:
www.rogerebert.com
www.theguardian.com/film
www.rottentomatoes.com
www.metacritic.com

## Chapter 9

Icarus story as told by Ovid in Book VIII of his *Metamorphoses*:
www.gutenberg.org/files/26073/26073-h/Met_VIII-XI.html#bookVIII_fableIII
Modern version of the Icarus story, still in copyright:
ovid.lib.virginia.edu

Traditional interpretation of the painting *The Raft of the Medusa* by Théodore Géricault:
artandperception.com/2007/10/gericaults-the-raft-of-the-medusa-by-tree.html
Modern reworking of the painting *The Raft of the Medusa* by Kara Walker:
blog.art21.org/2007/08/23/kara-walkers-art-graces-new-yorker-cover/#.U9N5Hq6_4ig

The painting *Gassed* by John Singer Sargent: www.iwm.org.uk/collections/item/object/23722
The painting *We Are Making a New World* by Paul Nash: www.bbc.co.uk/history/trail/wars_conflict/art/art_frontline_03.shtml
The painting *The Screened Road to 'A'* by AY Jackson: www.canadianmysteries.ca/sites/thomson/images/site/356058_2.jpg

Illustration of Act II, Scene I from Shakespeare's *Othello* (including Othello, Desdemona, Iago, Cassio, Emilia and Rodrigo):
www.georgeglazer.com/prints/aanda/art-pre20/boydell.html

Musical versions of *Full Fathom Five* from Shakespeare's *The Tempest*:
www.youtube.com/watch?v=3o6Lzl24u7w
www.youtube.com/watch?v=r4RJoD-RMhY

Videos of musical settings of Robert Frost's poem *Stopping by Woods on a Snowy Evening* by Randall Thompson:
www.youtube.com/watch?v=E3bUzZmoIRA
www.youtube.com/watch?v=T7c5c5DHGDc

Musical settings of the poem *Stopping by Woods on a Snowy Evening* by Robert Frost:
www.youtube.com/watch?v=hNwQxnIYD8k
www.youtube.com/watch?v=X4BIt0yq218